"Sarah Renee Werner has written a book that reaches us right where we live. Teaching us to live differently is our only path to healing. I highly recommend you make reading *Rooted Faith* a priority, and soon."

RANDY WOODLEY, author of *Becoming Rooted: One Hundred Days of Reconnecting with Sacred Earth*

"This book is a winsome, accessible meditation on creation as the environmental crisis looms over us. It lives at the intersection of gospel faith, Indigenous religion, and the earthly reality of belonging to and with and for the earth. The concrete focus on lived reality is evident as we learn that the 'dove' at the baptism of Jesus was a 'Palestinian pigeon,' and as we practice 'earthing'—that is, walking in bare feet to let our bodies feel the life-giving surges of the earth. A bonus of the book is an introduction to a wide literature on the subject, which is new to me. This is a fine, generative, suggestive read that remains focused on the reality of our earthly placement."

WALTER BRUEGGEMANN, William Marcellus McPheeters Professor Emeritus of Old Testament at Columbia Theological Seminary

"*Rooted Faith* is a timely field guide for getting to know God by getting outdoors. With passion and practical know-how, Sarah Renee Werner helps reconnect Christians who love the Creator with his glorious creation. We don't need more wonders in the world—just a greater sense of wonderment!"

MATTHEW SLEETH, MD, executive director of Blessed Earth and author of *Reforesting Faith* and *24/6*

"Winsome and wise, *Rooted Faith* provides a friendly entry point for Christians seeking to understand better and go deeper into Christian faithfulness at a time of planetary crisis. Sarah Renee Werner's emphasis on simple practices will be especially appealing for those who are ready to begin, but don't know how. For such readers, Werner offers a gracious invitation: it's okay—begin here."

DEBRA RIENSTRA, author of *Refugia Faith: Seeking Hidden Shelters, Ordinary Wonders, and the Healing of the Earth*

"'Christianity in its biblical roots is grounded in the earth,' argues Sarah Renee Werner in this refreshing and readable introduction to Christian creation care/earth spirituality/ecotheology. Churches must recover an interrelationship with a living biosphere, healing our de-formation by the objectification, dualism, and placelessness of settler colonialism by returning to the animist cosmology, poetic imagination, and incarnational geocentricism that are—surprise!—intrinsic to our scriptural narratives. She commends spiritual practices of reembodiment throughout to deepen personal and political wholeness and hope. An ideal book group resource!"

CHED MYERS, coauthor of *Healing Haunted Histories: A Settler Discipleship of Decolonization*

ROOTED FAITH

SARAH RENEE WERNER

ROOTED FAITH

PRACTICES *for* **LIVING WELL**
on a **FRAGILE PLANET**

HERALD
PRESS

Harrisonburg, Virginia

Herald Press
PO Box 866, Harrisonburg, Virginia 22803
www.HeraldPress.com

Library of Congress Cataloging-in-Publication Data
Names: Werner, Sarah Renee, author.
Title: Rooted faith : practices for living well on a fragile planet / Sarah
    Renee Werner.
Description: Harrisonburg, Virginia : Herald Press, [2023] | Includes
    bibliographical references.
Identifiers: LCCN 2023015467 (print) | LCCN 2023015468 (ebook) | ISBN
    9781513813165 (paperback) | ISBN 9781513813172 (hardcover) | ISBN
    9781513813189 (ebook)
Subjects: LCSH: Human ecology--Religious aspects--Christianity. | Christian
    stewardship. | BISAC: RELIGION / Christian Living / Social Issues |
    NATURE / Ecology
Classification: LCC BV772 .W434 2023 (print) | LCC BV772 (ebook) | DDC
    241/.691--dc23/eng/20230628
LC record available at https://lccn.loc.gov/2023015467
LC ebook record available at https://lccn.loc.gov/2023015468

Study guides are available for many Herald Press titles at www.HeraldPress.com.

27 26 25 24 23   10 9 8 7 6 5 4 3 2 1

To my parents,
for always supporting my creative endeavors

CONTENTS

FOREWORD

I fell in love with this book on the first page of the introduction. I seldom encounter a clear-eyed discussion of climate realities that is simultaneously grounded in rich and deep theology. That alone would have been enough to kindle my enthusiasm. But this book also offers pragmatic hope—not a starry-eyed optimism, but paths to explore that take us into our own bodies and their connection to the world around us and reorient our perspectives through daily actions and practices. This book is a potent antidote to despair, which inevitably leads to inaction and becomes a self-fulfilling prophecy. In *Rooted Faith: Practices for Living Well on a Fragile Planet*, Sarah Renee Werner invites us to remember that Christianity is, at its heart, a countercultural movement, and calls us to a new way of being in the world—or perhaps an old way that is worth rediscovering. This book offers a way of living that is rooted not in deprivation, but in wholeness, that we might have life, and have it abundantly.

We have come to a point in history when cynicism is often equated with realism, and where hope is conflated with naïveté. In the face of global pandemic, rapid and significant climate change, political upheaval, and so much more, it is easy to slip into despair. But despair is simply not a valid option.

Hope is no guarantee that our actions will bring about the changes we seek, but it is a prerequisite for action, and our participation in efforts to stem climate change and create a sustainable and equitable future together is desperately needed. Werner reminds us that it is faithful, practical, and realistic to show up for this work, and that the work can be joyful and healing even as it confronts toxic systems.

Václav Havel, the poet, playwright, activist, and former president of the Czech Republic, is often quoted as having said that "hope is not prognostication. It is an orientation of the spirit." It is not about what we think is going to happen. It is about where we point our lives. In choosing that direction, it is helpful to have good mentors. Though she is many years younger than I am, Werner has proven to be a wise mentor for me. "There is much to mourn on our planet," she writes,

> but there are also signs of hope, signs that humans are liv-
> ing into a more just and equitable future. This isn't to say
> that the future is bound to be rosy and perfect, and for
> those living in a war zone or under oppressive social sys-
> tems, all the statistics in the world cannot lessen the suffer-
> ing they experience. But something pivotal happens when
> we can sit with our grief long enough to realize that God is
> present in all times and places, and that, even in the midst
> of ongoing tragedy, there is beauty and joy and wonder.

In offering practical strategies for engagement, Werner does not forget that for this effort to truly bring about meaningful, lasting change, it must be personally sustainable and practiced in community. We are encouraged in these pages to constantly engage with wonder, and with the people around us, and to care for our own bodies, which are also a treasured part of God's creation.

The work ahead is daunting, to be sure, but there is reason for hope, and it is found in these pages.

—David LaMotte
Author of *You Are Changing the
World Whether You Like It or Not*

INTRODUCTION

I was a lanky, thoughtful sixteen-year-old growing up in Texas when, at a used bookstore, I stumbled upon a cookbook called *More-with-Less Cookbook,* by Doris Janzen Longacre. I was newly vegetarian and looking for meals to make for myself, trying to assert a newfound independence and identity. In its pages I found so much more than new recipes to try. First published in 1976 by Herald Press in cooperation with Mennonite Central Committee, *More-with-Less* was a call for Christians to live out their faith in the global community by eating in a way that used fewer of the world's resources. Longacre not only advocated eating more whole grains, legumes, and fruits and less meat and processed foods—she questioned the dominant economic order. I was in heaven.

Growing up awash in the consumer culture of a big city in a big oil state, I always felt like a bit of an odd duck. I was interested in camping and birds, in being alone in nature, but I was surrounded by the strip-mall landscape of urban sprawl that was North Texas in the late 1990s. And my church was not a place where cultural norms were being challenged. I absorbed Longacre's words like manna from heaven, and I wondered about these people called Mennonites, who lived so counter-culturally. Now, over twenty years later, I am a Mennonite pastor. It wasn't only the cookbook that eventually led me to the Mennonites, but it was my first glimpse of a Christian religious movement whose members truly sought to live more peacefully on the earth.

Longacre's call to live differently has stuck with me. I have not fully succeeded—I have come to realize that we are all too deeply enmeshed in our dominant extractive culture to entirely break free. But I have tried to consume less, to weigh my choices carefully, to walk instead of drive, to eat foods low on the food chain. I continue to grow more interested in how "ordinary Christians" are living out the call to dwell more peacefully and gently on the earth. Ideas are important, for sure, but ideas alone don't lead to substantive change. Actions do.

This is a book about what I believe to be the future of the church called to live differently—one of reinhabiting our particular landscapes and confronting the assumptions of consumer culture head-on through our lives and actions. This book is not just for fellow Mennonites but for all Christians. Though our unique theological traditions are important, this is a book about putting our faith into action through tangible practices. Mennonite traditions of peacebuilding and questioning the assumptions of the dominant culture have shaped my beliefs and thoughts, but neither of these values belongs exclusively to Mennonites. I believe that these ideas and practices can be a resource to you and your faith community as you seek to follow the example of Jesus and live more gently on our fragile planet.

THE CHALLENGE OF LIVING DIFFERENTLY ON A FRAGILE PLANET

As a Christian and an environmentalist, I see two consistent tension points continue to surface that can help us understand why it's so difficult to live differently—to live *well*—on our fragile planet. First, the Bible's call to live differently is in direct opposition to how our modern consumer culture encourages us to live. While North American culture places a premium on individual freedom and autonomy—on doing whatever we think will most benefit ourselves, when and how we feel like it—the Bible as a whole emphasizes that we ought to be concerned with and work toward the common good, including creating just economic systems and refraining from ostentatious wealth. The ideal society the Bible envisions, in both the Old and New Testament, is built on an economy of gifts and mutual aid.

The global capitalist system is the exact opposite, built on the continual accumulation of wealth by the few at the expense of the many. And as we see more with every passing year, this has direct consequences not only for those not born into privilege, but also for the earth itself. This is the natural outworking of our current limited framework, which places humans on top, as the pinnacle of creation. But the biblical vision of shalom points to a community of creation in which human lives are interwoven, dependent on the earth and on one another for all their needs.

Jesus, who spent his entire ministry as a homeless wanderer traveling from place to place and spreading a gospel message of a restored kingdom (or kin-dom),[1] embodied this beautiful vision. Looking at him we can see what it means to live differently on a fragile planet. He urged his followers to give away their wealth and to keep virtually nothing for themselves. He preached of a time to come when all who were hungry and thirsty would be fed, when the haughty would be made low and the poor would have what they need to survive. The Lord's Prayer, our most basic shared statement of faith, is a manifestation of this vision of a kin-dom of shalom: daily bread, forgiveness of debts, and an earthly order that mirrors that of heaven, a place for all to thrive, including the natural world. The early church took up this same message, sharing all goods in common and caring for every person. The apostle Paul paints a vision of a restored cosmos throughout his letters, a peace and a healing that go beyond the human community to include the groaning earth itself.

We find this vision in the Old Testament as well, from the Jubilee laws in Leviticus to the fiery words of the prophets. God desires justice and equality, the well-being of all creatures, not the adoration of kings. The earth was created for peace and harmony, not for subjugation and destruction. When the people inevitably fail to live up to this mandate, God speaks through the voices of prophets like Isaiah and Jeremiah, who call out the powerful ones and lay out a vision of a creation where the lion and the lamb can coexist in peace, where each being has its basic needs met. In Job and the Psalms we hear of the beauty and holiness of the wild species of the earth, created for the joy of God, not for any human ends. We forget all of this when we buy into the consumer culture's message of constant striving and desire for more stuff, despite the cost to others.

The second tension that can help us understand what makes it so difficult to live well on a fragile planet is this: though the world is full of beauty, it is also full of tragedy. Daily news reports make it feel like we're living in a world on fire. Many Indigenous people already feel the effects of climate change as they are forced from ancestral lands because of flooding or drought. For those living on the margins of our society, wildfires, hurricanes, and extreme heat can literally be life-ending. Climate change is the universal threat to every living being on the planet, but there is no doubt that it affects some more than others, and social and economic injustice only compound the problem.

Lasting change is only possible when we examine the roots of oppression, including the forced removal of Indigenous people in North America and the presence of environmental racism. The reality is that many people of color are impacted disproportionately by pollution, hazardous waste, and climate change. For this work to be sustainable in the long term, we have to figure out how to hold joy and tragedy together in tension, to make space for both lament and rejoicing in the miracle of life. Though injustice is woven into the fabric of our society, at least in North America, there are also hopeful signs of change everywhere, if we know where to look for them: the growing popularity of reusable items, the popularity of electric cars, and the concerted effort by many of the world's governments to address climate change and protect the planet's most vulnerable people.

But taking time to experience joy and wonder seems like a luxury we can't afford, or one we have during once-a-year vacations to faraway places, if we're fortunate enough to be able to take vacations at all. Many of us suffer an acute lack of joy and wonder in our daily lives, moving swiftly from one appointment to the next. The busier you are, our culture tells us, the more valuable you must be. Any free time should be filled up with useful activities, like laundry or paying bills. Closely related: the capitalist maxim that more stuff equals more happiness. We work harder to be able to afford more stuff, but once we get the objects of our desire, they turn out to not bring us the happiness we were hoping for. So, we work harder still to afford the next thing—a car, a house, a pool, a bigger car.

Don't misunderstand me: opening oneself up to joy and wonder is not the same thing as a constant starry-eyed optimism about the state of the world. Often the state of the world feels pretty dire. Daily news images offer a grim reality: war, mass shootings, and institutional racism. In North America, we have a long way to go before we get to anything even resembling justice and equity. But countless committed individuals are working to bend the arc of the moral universe toward justice—including climate justice—every day.

The easiest response to this daily onslaught of stressful information is to tune it out, to put one's head in the sand. But there are lots of actions, small and large, that can help avoid the worst of the damage. For every story of environmental catastrophe, there are five other untold ones about work that ordinary people are doing to change the world for the better. There's even a new generation of young people who are spreading that message on social media to encourage us to break out of our doom and gloom mindset and actually do something. In fact, climate change is the number one priority for many young people in the world today.[2] This makes sense, as they are the ones who will be living on this planet the longest; they do not want to inherit a trash heap.

This generation of climate advocates has recently spread their positive message on TikTok under the heading "OK Doomer." Playing off the "OK Boomer" meme—which challenges things older people say about the problems created by younger people—"OK Doomer" has become a rallying cry of those who oppose the paralyzing guilt we all experience when exposed to too much bad news about the earth. The easy way out is to give up and sink into inaction, believing that nothing we do will make a difference in the face of climate change. These young people are highlighting others who are making their communities better with community gardens, tree-planting projects, and other examples of effective environmental advocacy.

These experiences of joy and wonder in connecting to the natural world—not data and statistics—will lead people to change their actions and take better care of the earth. Watching fireflies dancing at night, seeing sea turtles hatch from a nest in the sand under a bright moon in midsummer—experiences of awe like these lead us to the sacred realm of life and help us feel our tiny insignificance as well as our immense value of being made in God's image. The natural world is full of wonder—even in the most urban park—all you have to do is put a magnifying glass in the hands of a child and watch that child examine ants and mosses and butterflies. When we take time to be still in the presence of God, we begin to be aware of how small we are in a large and beautiful world.

In an op-ed for *The New York Times* entitled "The Second Coming of the Lord God Bird" in the spring of 2022, nature writer Margaret Renkl wrote about a probable sighting of the ivory-billed woodpecker—once thought to be extinct, now potentially alive deep in a Louisiana forest. Renkl argued that what we love about stories like these is the idea that not all hope is lost. There is still the possibility for redemption. She pointed to recent costly legislation to protect wilderness areas passed in Tennessee and Florida as evidence that environmental issues are becoming more widely accepted as a priority. In the case of Florida, the act passed with a unanimous vote in both the Senate and House. Protecting the environment has suddenly become popular.

There is danger, of course, in this newfound popularity—greenwashing, or the practice of marketing a product as environmentally friendly when it is perhaps only slightly better than other products but still quite far from actually being good for the environment. This perception can easily convince people they're doing something good and keep them from taking more drastic and necessary actions.

But there is a great deal of movement happening in all corners of the country when it comes to climate change. For example, sales of electric vehicles are up. As I write this, California, the most populous state in the country, recently ran solely on renewable energy for a day.[3] Many consumers can now opt to get their power from renewable energy sources. Bike lanes are popping up everywhere in North America, and cyclists are making use of them. Chances are high that you live within easy driving distance of a farmers market, the best place to buy food locally and support your area farmers directly.[4] There is hope, yet, that we may embrace the call to live differently on this fragile planet of ours.

THE ROLE OF THE CHURCH

In an intriguing parallel to the conversation about the future of our planet, there is a great deal of anxiety about trying to discern the future of the Christian tradition. Some have said the church is dying out. Others have argued for its renewal, with a variety of solutions. Some have said the future of the church is green. Others have pointed out that many churches are moving in the opposite direction, shunning climate change, science, and modern culture altogether. Christianity is so varied globally that it's difficult to generalize. This book is not meant to speak for all Christians or to speak on behalf of some monolith of Christianity as a single institution. Christianity is and always has been a highly varied, multicultural, multilingual religion.

But one thing is clear: churches have a pivotal role to play in addressing both of these challenges—in calling ourselves and our communities to live differently. And the church's actions could help set the future directions for both the planet and the church. We are standing at the crossroads between our inherited culture and the biblical vision of shalom.

There is no doubt that the church, and religion in society more generally, is in the midst of a massive change. Some churches are dying out, but others are growing, and many of the growing ones tend to emphasize social justice and creation care. These are the prescient concerns of our world today. If churches want to grow, they need to be listening to the concerns of the younger generation, and youth's overwhelming message is that they care about the earth, about other people, and about their own future in this perilous place. They care about how all of us are living out what we believe, about how our lives and communities are transformed by the call to live differently.

My own congregation is growing consistently each year. People joining our congregation care about the work we do together—housing refugees, dismantling racism, confronting our complicity as a majority-white, middle-class congregation, working for peace in our community and throughout the world, learning to inhabit our unique place in the landscape. As someone who works with young people, I see that they are terrified of what everyone is doing to the planet and angry that the adults in power seem entirely unmotivated to address the problems that will affect their future. They know what crisis feels like—hurricanes, tornadoes, school shootings, a pandemic—and they know we're only headed for more pain the longer we try to uphold the status quo. Youth need to hear a clear message from their religious tradition: that someone cares enough about them, about the earth, and about our collective future to live differently.

Something fundamental has broken in society. We have realized that not just our individual actions but our culture has to change. This is the gift that the last three years of pandemic living has given us. Things cannot continue as they have, and we are the ones who have the power to change them. For thousands of species, it's already too late, and we must grieve for all that we have lost. The gospel message is clear that we should do all we can to build the kin-dom of heaven on earth.

CORE SEEDS OF WISDOM

On this journey together, we will consider some core seeds of wisdom as we explore what it means to live well on our fragile planet, in solidarity with our human and non-human neighbors. **First is the importance of understanding that everything is alive,** but our modern way of life makes us numb to this reality. Many of us spend a good portion of our lives indoors, moving from one space to another in the climate-controlled comfort of vehicles. Time spent outside is a luxury some cannot afford, and many others feel constantly pressed for time between commitments to family, coworkers, and other responsibilities. But when we make time to step outside and be still in nature, whether it is in a city park, on a beach, or on an open prairie, something shifts inside. Witnessing birds chirping, water gurgling, and trees rustling in the breeze, we begin to remember that we are part of a larger universe that is bursting with vibrant life.

As we become aware of the life of the universe of which we are but a small part, it is helpful to remember that **the Bible was written by people with a dramatically different awareness of the world around them,** a world at once pulsing with life and full of danger and uncertainty. Scripture shows the reality of thoroughly premodern cultures, where most people lived in intimate connection with the landscape around them. They were concerned about the well-being of the harvest and about whether the rain would fall in its season or their crops would be damaged by drought or pests. The Old Testament reflects a people intricately bound up in the land, with laws that make clear that God is the ultimate owner and humans are merely tenants on it. In the New Testament, Jesus lived most of his life outside, traveling from town to town during his ministry, accompanied at times by disciples, but also living among the wild animals during his sojourns. This is reflected in the gospel parables about sheep, wheat, seeds, weeds, and other agricultural images that would have been well-known to his audience. In order to truly understand the biblical vision of shalom, a creation characterized by wholeness and peace, we have to wrap our minds around the animate worldview of these ancient peoples.

A faithful reading of the Bible entails reconnecting with this sense of aliveness, to root ourselves in the joy and wonder of the natural world. Since Jesus' ministry mainly took place in fields and beside lakeshores, we ought to read scripture with an embodied sense of the vibrant landscape in our minds. There are many ways to tap into the vibrancy of the natural world, including meditation, going on a nature walk, having worship outdoors, and many others. When we reconnect with the earth, we gain a deeper understanding of the context in which the Bible was written.

Heading out into the wide world—into the wilderness or to the heart of the city—also opens us up to the awareness of how much hurt exists. From systemic racism to habitat loss, there is a lot to mourn when we open our eyes to the plight of creation. This leads to a third seed of wisdom: **emotions are important,** and we can feel the whole gamut of them when it comes to facing the climate crisis. Once we open ourselves up to noticing what is happening in the world around us, we cannot help but see the devastating effects that the climate crisis has wrought on both human and non-human life. The evidence is all around us, and it is painful to behold: children poisoned by toxic runoff from mining operations, endangered species on the brink of extinction, rising sea levels encroaching on vulnerable human communities.

When we come to terms with grieving and lamenting what we have lost, our hearts can break open with love for all beings, and we realize that **we are always intimately connected to the land and the human communities around us.** The local and the global realms permeate one another. Our way of life directly harms others, near and far. The natural gas that heats my home in the winter likely has come from fracking in Pennsylvania or West Virginia, an extraction process that can taint the well water of nearby farms. My life is necessarily bound up with millions of other lives, linked by networks of goods and systems of power. We are never just ourselves alone and isolated. This also means that when we make positive changes in our own lives, these ripple out to the rest of the world, even if they might seem small and insignificant.

And finally, **to be truly alive is to feel all of this and to work for the restoration of creation,** to connect to the earth, and to connect with the Sacred that suffuses all of it. This is our role as Christians, to root ourselves in our places and open our hearts to the joy and tragedy around us, knowing that God is present in all of it. In the book of Revelation, the hope of a new heaven and new earth refers to a restored earth right where we are, not in some otherworldly realm. The heart of what it means to be Christian is to work to foster the kin-dom of God in the places where we live, with our eyes open to all the beauty and suffering around us.

To live well on this fragile planet, we need a renewed focus on living out our faith through tangible, everyday practices, along with a shift in our modern, capitalist worldview that places financial gain above all else.

In the chapters that follow, I will explore this new framework for living out our faith, one that is grounded in our particular place on this sacred earth. Each chapter is centered on a biblical text that invites us into a new way of seeing ourselves in relationship with the rest of creation. Each chapter also includes one or more practices for opening our hearts to both the beauty and tragedy around us and guiding us toward meaningful action to restore creation.

So join me as we remember our place in "the family of things," to use the words of Mary Oliver, to find a way into true aliveness.[5] Life is uncertain and sometimes perilous, and we can't always protect ourselves and our loved ones from pain and loss. But we find wholeness by being present through all of life and in recognizing that God can be found in every crevice of the universe.

Chapter 1

ALL CREATION IS ALIVE

Make a joyful noise to the LORD, *all the earth;*
  break forth into joyous song and sing praises. . . .
Let the sea roar, and all that fills it;
  the world and those who live in it.
Let the floods clap their hands;
  let the hills sing together for joy
at the presence of the LORD, *for he is coming*
  to judge the earth.
He will judge the world with righteousness,
  and the peoples with equity. (Psalm 98:4, 7–9)

Early spring is always an amazing time in Ohio, as a succession of gorgeous wildflowers, beginning with snowbells and crocus, sprout up from the frozen ground. Then come the daffodils in front gardens and trout lilies with their mottled waxy leaves and delicate yellow flowers along the streambanks. Finally in late March, the slender white flowers of the trillium appear deep in the forest, a vivid reminder of the brilliance of creation. If you're not paying attention, though, it's easy to miss this brilliant display of life springing up.

The whole world is practically bursting with this kind of life, but often our fascination with technology and desire for comfort numbs us to this reality. We walk around with head-phones in our ears, not hearing the melodic songs of the birds in our neighborhoods. We travel from one place to another in the artificial comfort of vehicles, barely seeing the landscape as it moves past our window. How much do you know about the plants and animals in the landscape you inhabit? Do you recognize the birds that flit in and out of the trees? Do you live in a place where the sky unfolds with stars each night, and if so, do you know the names of the constellations written in the velvet black sky overhead? Part of living well on a fragile planet is reconnecting to this most basic type of knowledge, orienting ourselves in relation to the beings around us. This is also the knowledge those living in biblical times would have carried with them, knowledge that connected them to the Creator.

Our love of technology and commitment to comfort make it almost impossible to see the aliveness of the world around us. This was not true for the biblical writers and the original audience of the scriptures—their lives and bodies were intrinsically connected to the earth, to the landscapes and the creatures around them. This shaped their understanding of the value of the natural world, of their purpose in it, and of God, who gives and breathes life.

It is only when we see the life around us that we can begin to value it, and it is only when we value it that we can begin to live well in and among these other beings. Each of us was born into a particular landscape that has shaped us, even if we're half a world away from where we started out. We can begin to reconnect to our place by simply going outside and opening all of our senses to the world around us. This doesn't have to mean wandering out into the middle of the wilderness—we can wake up wherever we are, on an urban city block, a suburban lawn, or beside a meandering neighborhood stream.

It is only when we wake up to the life around us that we can fully connect with the Holy Spirit, the One who suffuses the universe. Paying attention can help us feel closer to God and to the community of creation, as well. And reading the Bible with an eye toward the value God places in a sentient creation is a reclamation of the heart of Jesus for all created things—shaped by Creator God. The Bible shows a worldview that we have lost in our headlong dive into a technologically-mediated reality. By grounding ourselves in our own landscape, we can tap into this deeper connection with God and creation and begin to understand what it means to live well on a fragile planet. This is important because those of us immersed in the consumer culture of the modern West are not taught to value the rest of creation as much as we value the needs and desires of humankind. The earth and all its inhabitants are mere resources for us to use wisely. But once we begin to connect to the natural world, learning to name the plants and animals around us, we become a part of a holy creation much larger than ourselves and we realize that the vibrant life of earth exists for its own benefit, not for ours. It is this perspective that characterizes much of the biblical texts, especially the psalms.

THE CREATION OF A SENTIENT WORLD

As we seek to wake up to the life around us, we can begin with Psalm 98—a hymn that proclaims an awake and alive earth. In it, the whole earth is encouraged to praise God, and the writer describes in detail how each aspect of creation contributes to the song—from the ocean waves to the hills. It is so antithetical to how we view creation in the modern Western mindset that we often read right past these words, dismissing them as simply metaphor or hyperbole. Surely the ocean cannot praise God; it's just water moving with currents and wind. And what is more unmoving than a mountain? This underscores how our worldview keeps us from living well; it puts forth the human mind as the only thinking being in the universe, alone in a vast web of ecosystems that all run based on the determined principles of evolution. This is a distinctly Western way of thinking about the world; for Indigenous people throughout the world, the idea that oceans and mountains think and act and have their own life force is an obvious fact, one that shapes a very different approach to what it means to live well on a fragile planet.

In his book *Becoming Animal*, environmental philosopher David Abram recounts a story that can help us begin to see the creatures and forms of the earth as alive and exerting their effects on us. He takes the reader on an imaginary journey, describing a walk down a winding narrow path toward a stream. He describes the sound of frogs, the steady gurgle of the water, and then asks the reader to imagine rounding the corner to see a cliff suddenly towering above: "The cliff leans far over the stream, eclipsing most of the sky. As your eyes travel up its face, I watch your mouth drop open, and see your knees bend as you drop to a crouch."[1] After marveling at the intricate details of its rock face, Abram continues by engaging in a theoretical dialogue with the reader about how we often think of rocks only as unmoving features of the landscape. In fact, he points out, they exert a certain pull over us, as evidenced by our strong reaction when coming upon the tall cliff face in the forest. Rocks move us in a real sense. Abram ends the passage with a bold assertion: "The stillness, the quietude of this rock is its very activity, the steady gesture by which it enters and alters your life."[2]

This concept—that there is much more life that is awake and aware on the earth than merely humans—is called animism.

The term *animism* was originally used by British anthropologist E. B. Tylor to pejoratively describe the religious worldview of Indigenous peoples who ascribed a spirit to all things, in opposition to the "pure monotheism" of the religions of so-called civilized cultures, namely Judaism and Christianity. Tylor and other scholars wanted to justify colonialism by denigrating the views of colonized peoples, pinning animism to a "primitive" superstition that ought to be superseded by science and the modern enlightenment. This definition has stuck, but it demonstrates the limits of a modern Western worldview that can only conceive of concepts like "spirit" or "alive" within the boundaries of a very narrow definition.

The term *animism* has recently been revived to describe a concept that recognizes that humans are not the only sentient and inspirited beings in the cosmos. Religion scholar Graham Harvey defines animists as "people who recognize that the world is full of persons, only some of whom are human, and that life is lived in relationship with others."[3] This is not at all in conflict with the Bible; in fact, this same idea is found throughout Scripture.[4] Animism was, in fact, the dominant worldview of the Jews at the time of Jesus and early Christianity. This earthy foundation was only extracted from these religions much later, in an attempt to be defined in opposition to the religion of the "uncivilized" people being colonized.[5]

The seemingly paradoxical term *Christian animism* has recently arisen in religious-studies circles to reclaim the biblical vision of a sentient and sacred cosmos. And understanding the animist context in which the Bible was written is not just a helpful method for reading passages like Psalm 98 well; looking back also helps us understand our own current situation with new awareness. When the psalmist writes that the oceans and the mountains praise God with their own voices, the text isn't written as metaphor or hyperbole—it's meant to tell us that mountains and oceans speak in their own ways and that we can hear them if only we are awake enough to listen.

This message echoes across Scripture; the Bible is clear that it is not only humans who have the ability to connect with God, but each organism in the universe communicates God's message. In the Genesis creation accounts, God is a brooding bird, hovering over the waters, and then the Divine Being walks in the garden of Eden with the humans. God wrestles in bodily form with Jacob in Genesis 32 and speaks through the burning bush in Exodus 3. In the prophetic literature, the well-being of the land is linked to the right actions of humans. The land is desecrated by human sin, seen most strongly in the murder of Abel in Genesis 4, when the blood cries out from the ground. In the book of Hosea, the land suffers because the people have turned away from God.[6] This matters because it makes clear that humans are not the only creatures with agency or the only beings that God cares about protecting. When we forget that we are only one among many created holy beings, we see the earth only as a backdrop for a human drama and as bounty free for the taking. This is not what God intends for us or for creation.

JESUS AND THE ANIMALS

The Old Testament isn't the only place where the sentience of creation is depicted. In the Gospels, Jesus shows an intimate knowledge of the landscape around him, and birds and storms alike play a role in the narrative. The New Testament narrative begins with Jesus' birth in a stable, where the farm animals are the first witnesses to the coming of the Christ child. We imagine Mary giving birth in the quiet company of goats, sheep, and cows, their soft bodies giving warmth to the dark space.

In Luke's account of Jesus' baptism by John in the Jordan River, the Holy Spirit takes the form of a dove. In a direct translation by religion scholar Mark Wallace of Luke 3:22, "The Holy Spirit descended upon [Jesus] in bodily form [*somatiko eidei*], as a dove/pigeon [*hos preisteran*]."[7] The original Greek text is clear that this isn't allegory or symbolism; the Holy Spirit is embodied as a dove. The word used here, which is traditionally translated as *dove,* actually refers to the earthy Palestinian pigeon, a mottled brown and green creature closely related to the modern rock dove, which is endemic to city parks and streets the world over.

Immediately after his baptism, Jesus goes out into the wilderness, where the wild beasts wait on him. Mark, always the briefest with his words, takes space to note that while Jesus was tempted by Satan in the wilderness, "he was with the wild beasts; and the angels waited on him" (Mark 1:13). During this time of tribulation, it is wild creation and supernatural powers that sustain him. I can imagine Jesus befriending wild foxes and watching the path of the hawk across the sky as he struggled with the overwhelming reality of the work that lay ahead of him.

The parables of Jesus are filled with agricultural imagery: mustard seeds, wheat and chaff, fig trees, lost sheep, and sparrows of the field. These images speak to a culture that was intimately connected to the land and the changes of each season. When Jesus said that the kingdom of God is like a mustard seed, it helps to know that mustard is one of the tiniest seeds, barely larger than a grain of sand, and yet if planted in good soil, it grows into a tree-like bush within a very short span of time.

These living beings weren't merely sermon illustrations; Jesus saw them as fellow creatures in a sacred world. His use of plants and animals as examples shows us we can learn a great deal about God by observing the organisms in the landscape around us. "Look at the birds of the air; they neither sow nor reap nor gather into barns, and yet your heavenly Father feeds them," Jesus exhorted his followers in Matthew 6:26. Just after this he said, "Consider the lilies of the field, how they grow; they neither toil nor spin, yet I tell you, even Solomon in all his glory was not clothed like one of these" (Matthew 6:28–29). The message is clear: birds and flowers are sentient beings that God cares for just as God cares for humans. We are just one of many valuable creations on this earth.

During his ministry, after healing people and speaking to large crowds, Jesus frequently retreated to the wilderness to restore himself, taking refuge on lakeshores and mountaintops. In *When God Was a Bird*, Mark Wallace poetically observes that "Jesus' mission emerged, therefore, from his deep communion with landed places integral to his daily peregrinations. His identity with spiritually saturated thin places entailed as well his sense of belonging with trees and flowers, wind-blown seas, and the starry atmosphere above."[8]

The messages that Jesus sought to impart during his life reflected this close relationship with the land, developed through a life spent traveling primarily on foot. He offered most of his teachings in outdoor areas rather than in synagogues. Jesus chose the side of a mountain as the place from which to deliver his most well-known extended teaching, the Sermon on the Mount (Matthew 5:1–2). At the end of his life, Jesus sought refuge in a garden, and this is also where Mary first saw him on the morning of his resurrection. Gardens can be wilderness refuges in the middle of cities, places full of green life. It seems fitting that Jesus would have spent his last night alive in a garden, and that Mary would mistake him for a gardener when he was newly resurrected.

ANTIDOTES TO AN OTHERWORLDLY THEOLOGY: INDIGENOUS AND CELTIC PERSPECTIVES

How did we lose this animate worldview that runs so clearly through the biblical text? When the Emperor Constantine converted to Christianity in the fourth century CE, the religion became more mainstream in Rome, officially becoming the state religion in 380 with the Edict of Thessalonica. In this identity shift from a religion of the oppressed to the religion of the empire, certain elements that might threaten the status quo were downplayed or suppressed—specifically the affirmation of the leadership roles of women, the emphasis on social equality and communal living, and the recognition of the land as belonging to God.

The emphasis on personal salvation—often to the neglect of the common good—became even more extreme in the late nineteenth century, when fundamentalism and millennialism rose in popularity in Western culture. Cultivating personal piety and getting into heaven became more important than responding with charity and justice in a hurting world. Fundamentalism was in part a reaction to the rising influence of Charles Darwin's evolutionary theory and a growing awareness of the risk this posed to the prevailing Christian understanding of the earth's origins. Even the more progressive Protestant churches focused on the plight of humanity while excluding that of the natural world, emphasizing the need for social justice but not expanding their caring to other species. And each of these traditions downplayed the Bible's emphasis on relationship with place and land to instead preach Christianity as a faith for all people everywhere, a universal culture.

Christian tradition, however, has from its beginning been much broader than the dominant theology. The Eastern Orthodox Church has always been much more rooted in the earth and embodied practices than the Roman Catholic Church; the current leader Bartholomew has been dubbed the Green Patriarch. Celtic Christianity, too, has a deep rootedness in creation. When Celtic missionaries began landing on foreign shores, some of the cultures they encountered absorbed the Jesus way into their own naturalistic worldview, creating numerous expressions of place-based and culturally diverse streams of Christianity.

The roots of the Celtic Christian tradition stretch back to the fourth century CE, when the first Christians arrived in the British Isles and Ireland. For its first two hundred years, Celtic Christianity developed without interference from the Roman Church, which led to its great respect for the natural world and emphasis on the goodness of the body and of creation. These believers saw the gospel as a natural extension of pre-Christian Celtic beliefs and practices. Early Celtic Christian communities "worshipped without temples in the wild, in forests and on mountains" rather than in buildings, wanting to be closer to God's creation.[9]

During this same period, the Roman Church grew increasingly intertwined with political power, eventually making its way to the British Isles and bringing with it its emphasis on the doctrine of original sin and the fallen nature of humans and the created world. The idea of original sin was important for upholding the tenets of political systems because it supported the notion that the deepest nature of humans (and creation) was sinful and corrupt, in need of salvation from God. This allowed the empire to value humans and the created world in a relative way, only as worthy once they had been redeemed, not as intrinsically valuable and holy creations of God from their beginnings. While the Synod of Whitby in 664 officially established the Roman Church as the presiding tradition in the

British Isles, Celtic Christian beliefs and practices continued to some degree even into the twentieth century, surviving official censure of the Roman Church, the Protestant Reformation and subsequent Calvinism of the British Isles, and the Scottish Highland Clearances in the nineteenth century.[10]

Celtic Christianity has persevered and its focus on the goodness of creation and the light of God in each person is a powerful antidote to the soul-crushing, humanity-denying worldview of industrial and post-industrial Europe, where people are merely cogs in the machine of capitalism. Even as rural Scots were cast out of their land during the Clearances and when thousands of Irish families starved during the potato famine, their life-affirming spirituality prevailed in songs, poems, and prayers, and it continues up to the present day. This is a testament to the power of an earth-centered faith and a choice to see the goodness in creation despite persecution.

Several key themes in the Celtic Christian tradition can help us reclaim the earth-centered worldview of the early Christians. In embracing the Celtic Christian emphasis on Christ as the light of the world, we rediscover a universe that is wholly suffused with the light of Christ. This theological idea is stated clearly in John 1:9: "The true light, which enlightens everyone, was coming into the world." We in the modern West have understood that light to relate primarily to humans and the human connection with the Divine, but that light was meant for all of creation. In *Sacred Earth, Sacred Soul*, scholar John Philip Newell writes, "In the Celtic world Christ is viewed not as coming to reveal a foreign truth but to disclose the deepest truth of our being."[11] This understanding shapes the contemplative Christian tradition, which draws its inspiration from the story in the gospel of John of the disciple reclining on the shoulder of Jesus and hearing his heartbeat during the Last

Supper. In stepping into this tradition, we too can learn to listen for the heartbeat of God in the world. That heartbeat, we
are reminded, can be found all around us thanks to the light
of Christ. Newell notes that when John begins his gospel with
the declaration that "In the beginning was the Word" (1:1),
and that all things had come into being through this Word
(1:3), the biblical author is saying "that essentially all life is an
expression of God. We have been uttered into being. To learn
of God, therefore, is to listen to the heart of life."[12]

Celtic Christianity also helps us appreciate God's grandeur
through its emphasis on *two* books of scripture—the Bible
and creation. Newell writes that "Celtic wisdom looks for the
flow of the divine deep within everything that has being. It
is like a subterranean river coursing through the veins of the
universe."[13] This tradition teaches that, because God is present
in all of creation, including within us, we can look for God
speaking to us through nature. What we hear from creation
then ought to be in conversation with what we read in the
Bible, and vice versa. Only then is it possible to appreciate the
true grandeur of God's work in the universe.

Understanding creation this way reframes the work of
Jesus as one who came not to deliver us from a sinful world,
but to remind us of this connection we forgot when humans
were cast out of the harmony of the garden of Eden. In the
words of Newell, Jesus shows us that we are "bearers of the
divine flow," and "reawakens us to our true nature and the
true nature of the earth, that we and all things are in essence
sacred." This can be seen both in the way that he lived his life
and in the lessons he shared about the kin-dom of God.[14]

When the wisdom of both Scripture and creation weaves
together in us—the truth of the history of God's presence with
a particular people in the Hebrew Scriptures and the vision of

restoration in the Gospels, together with the knowledge found in the vibrant, sentient earth all around us—we understand all of creation is suffused with holiness. This makes it possible to seek wisdom about God from both the Bible and the created world. Reclaiming this inheritance as part of our daily aware-ness is crucial for opening ourselves to the joy and wonder of being embedded in the natural world—a joy God intended for us all along.

Celtic Christians also believed in the essential goodness of the body and creation, an idea that is in direct opposition to the doctrine of original sin. We find these ideas articulated by Pelagius, a fifth-century Christian thinker best known by many as the opponent of St. Augustine of Hippo. Augustine argued against the need for grace in salvation, but Pelagius disagreed. Augustine, who disapproved of this Celtic focus on the goodness of the body and the sacredness of the created world, believed that humans were born flawed, in need of sal-vation to rescue them from their fallen nature. He believed that bodies were the source of sin and depravity and in need of controlling, not holy vessels of God's love.

In his opposition to the doctrine of original sin, which necessitates for our salvation a movement of the grace of God, Pelagius argued that the grace humans need is found within nature and within themselves—a gift of God from within, rather than from without. "Narrow shafts of divine light pierce the veil that separates heaven from earth," Pelagius wrote.[15] While in the sixth and seventh centuries Western Christianity was increasingly devoted to the doctrine of original sin, the Celtic and Eastern Orthodox churches continued to "celebrate that which is deepest in the newborn child, and thus at the heart of every woman and man, is the dignity of the divine."[16] Such a view threatened the iron grasp of the political powers, which treated both humans and the environment as tools to be used, not as sacred beings infused with holiness.

This view of human nature is important to the goal of living well on the earth because it recognizes human bodies as an integral part of creation. Acknowledging the goodness of our bodies helps us acknowledge the goodness of the created world. We, and the earth, are not sinful matter in need of redemption but beloved creations of God to be cherished.

This interrelationship of all things is echoed in the truths found in the ecological sciences. Famous naturalist John Muir captured it best in these words: "When we try to pick out anything by itself, we find it hitched to everything else in the universe."[17] The legacy of Celtic Christianity reminds us that there is no ultimate separation between humans and nature, between the eternal and the mundane, and everything is intertwined—God and humans and the abundant energy of the natural world.

Indigenous cultures all over the world responded similarly to hearing the gospel of Jesus by synthesizing Christian theology with their traditional, earth-based worldview. Randy Woodley, a theologian and member of the Keetoowah Nation (Cherokee), is one of many Indigenous Christian scholars who are eager to share their own version of a rooted faith. Woodley is both a teacher and a farmer, running an heirloom seed farm as part of the Eloheh Indigenous Center for Earth Justice in Oregon. *Eloheh* is a Cherokee word that translates roughly as balance or harmony way, and it represents both a place and a way of life.[18] Woodley was moved to share his Indigenous Christian faith with others because he hoped to offer a different perspective on Christianity that many Western Christians have lost. In his book *Shalom and the Community of Creation*, he writes, "There exists in America a ubiquitous and foundationally dualistic theology behind the idea of living between heaven and earth. As human beings, I think that both the Native American and the ancient Semitic view on the subject is that we are made to experience the fullness of our relationship *with* the earth and *on* the earth."[19]

Woodley compares the biblical vision of shalom with the Native American Harmony Way, the idea that life thrives in harmony and balance, and that loss of that balance results in disease and destruction. Through extensive interviews with Indigenous elders throughout North America, he identifies the Harmony Way as a hallmark of Native American spirituality.[20]

This concept aligns with the biblical concept of shalom, usually translated as "peace." The vision of shalom goes beyond the mere absence of conflict, pointing us toward the hope of a cosmos in total harmony with God.[21] We find this vision of shalom all over the Hebrew Bible, from the perfection of the garden of Eden to Isaiah's vision of the wolf laying down with the lamb (11:6–9). The book of Leviticus describes the Jubilee year, a practice of forgiving all debts and returning all property to its original owners, a practice that resets the economic order to ensure equity and justice for all inhabitants of the land. As Woodley notes, "Shalom is meant to be both personal (emphasizing our relationships with others) and structural (replacing systems where shalom has been broken or which produce broken shalom, such as war- or greed-driven economic systems."[22] Shalom is thus all of creation living in harmony in an interconnected web of sharing, and Woodley suggests that this way of living is found in so many traditional cultures because it is God's intended way for humans to live.[23]

Because shalom is concerned with the common good, it clashes with our culture of individualism and capitalist striving. Those of us who have benefitted from these systems feel

threatened by what shalom may mean for our personal inter-
ests. Embracing shalom requires us to reconfigure our understanding of what it means to live well. Theologian Walter
Brueggemann describes shalom as "well-being of a material,
physical, historical kind, not idyllic 'pie in the sky,' but salvation in the midst of trees and crops and enemies—in the
very places where people always have to cope with anxiety, to
struggle for survival, and to deal with temptation."[24]

Jesus embraced this vision of shalom when he began his
ministry, calling it the kingdom of God—including not just
humans but all of creation.[25] As Woodley points out, the term
kingdom offered to Jesus' original audience a forceful antidote
to the language of the empire, but today a more useful phrase
is that of the community of creation.[26] Jesus' parables and
healing miracles point to a vision of a restored creation, and
we have explored already how his teachings are mostly centered on the natural world. Woodley reminds us that, being a
carpenter, Jesus could have used mechanical terms in his teachings, but Jesus intentionally focused on agricultural imagery
like birds, crops, and fish because his worldview centered on
creation.[27] Yet, while Jesus spent his whole ministry talking to
the elements of the natural world around him, "most of us live
insulated from the conversation with creation that Jesus and
many of the biblical writers held daily."[28]

When we do not enter into that mutual conversation with
the land around us, we also miss out on something fundamental in the Bible, something Jesus modeled for us and offers to
us as a better way to live—a strong and implicit connection
with the natural world and a recognition that the earth is our
true home and the dwelling place of God.

We can only live well on this fragile planet when we live
in this kind of interrelated community. When we reframe

our understanding of creation in this way, our actions matter beyond how they affect us alone. We can only understand them as part of a web of relationships drawing us deeper into community—with our fellow humans, as we reject the idea that the goal of life is to gain more for ourselves at the expense of others, and also as we become more aware of our local landscape and its ecological limits.

As we pursue this kind of rooted faith, church communities have an important part to play in fostering this in their members. The words and symbols the church uses matter. They can create either an ethos of connection and care for the world or lead us to detach entirely from it in hope of some ethereal salvation elsewhere. In his teachings Jesus emphasized that heaven is something to be created here on earth (Matthew 6:10), so devoting ourselves to God is to devote ourselves to caring for the world around us.

Training our eyes to see this web of interconnection also trains us to see God's presence in all things. When I sit in my backyard and am captivated by the deer that grazes nearby and the hummingbird dancing among the tree branches, I feel enveloped by the Sacred. I see the light of God flowing through these animals and the trees and even the warm earth beneath my feet. In Newell's words, "the whole fabric of creation is woven through with the thread of God's light."[29]

SEARCHING FOR AN EARTHY, GROUNDED FAITH

I have lived my entire life enfolded in the Christian tradition, and I have been searching almost as long for an aspect of this tradition that roots me deeply in the landscape around me. I found little evidence of this in the Christianity of my childhood, but I kept looking. I knew that my powerful experiences encountering red-tailed hawks and great blue herons and other animals meant something. This deep impulse that we all have to feel the presence of the Sacred in daily life, to connect to the lifeforce of the universe, is also born from a desire to feel less alone, to feel bound up in a web of community both human and nonhuman.

When I was in seminary, I led a church group on a hike at Sweetwater Creek State Park near Atlanta, Georgia. It was early spring and the whole landscape felt vibrantly alive, over-flowing with a sense of the sacred, but I struggled with how to relate this presence of the holy to the biblical faith I had inherited. I knew a great deal about how Indigenous and New Age spirituality connected nature with the sacred realm of life, but I had never heard anyone talk about how the Bible might speak to my love of nature and the holy portents I saw in the presence of a red fox at the edge of the field or the tree sprouting up from barren ground. Only in the last few years have I started to recognize that the Bible is full of passages about how plants and animals emanate the sacredness of a holy creation, as oceans and prairies sing praises to the Holy One.

I am only now recovering the language of the ordinary holiness of life. The Bible is full of this imagery, but it has been lost in my culture's obsession with dominion, subjugation, and power. These values only leave us feeling isolated and alone—humans high on a pedestal, the pinnacle of creation—when the truth is that we are embedded in a web of community, both human and nonhuman, all shot through with holiness.

Nothing reminds me of this community more than my frequent interactions with a resident merlin that lives in my neighborhood. Merlins are small raptors in the falcon family that are typically found in Ohio only during migration. For whatever reason, this merlin has chosen my street as her year-round home. It's a good habitat as far as urban wilderness goes—it offers a plentiful supply of songbirds to eat in addition to mice and voles, as well as a whole forest of trees in which to take shelter. It feels like a particular blessing to have her here watching me, her small, feathered frame observing my comings and goings as she waits for the right moment to pounce on a house sparrow at a bird feeder or for a chipmunk to come sprinting across the grass. We sometimes sit and watch each other for minutes at a time, me stock still in the middle of the street and her on a low telephone line, eyeing me warily but not flying away. I know that crows have strong memories and can remember individual humans. I wonder if Merlin, as I have taken to calling her, remembers my face, the strange human who stops to watch her. Above all, it feels like a blessing to be seen by another animal, to be reminded that not all sentient beings are human, and to wonder how this small raptor experiences the creative flow of being alive.

My recognition of this bird's presence is possible because I have begun to cultivate an awareness of the sacred, a kind of lived prayer as I walk every day, helping me to be aware of this landscape of blessing. She reminds me of my sacred connection to the cosmos, just as the mourning doves cooing from the power line remind me of the embodied Holy Spirit. I observe the world, but the world is also watching me, alive and aware of more than I can fathom. I imagine that this is how Jesus saw the world around him as he traveled throughout the landscape of first-century Palestine, alive and full of meaning. We are never just ourselves alone.

PUTTING IT INTO PRACTICE: EARTHING

As we seek to develop this sense of the community of creation, we can look to the meditative practice of earthing. This is simply the practice of walking barefoot outdoors, either on the grass, along a beach, or on bare dirt. The idea behind earthing is that walking barefoot helps us tap into the well of electrons found in the earth, to bring about healing. A surprising amount of scientific research has found multiple health benefits from the practice of earthing, including lower levels of stress hormones, improved sleep, lower blood pressure, and decreases in cardiovascular disease.[30]

To engage in earthing, simply step outside and take your shoes off. Stand or walk on the ground, feeling the earth under your bare feet. If you are not able to stand or walk, you can sit in a chair with your bare feet in the grass and receive the same benefit. I have grown fond of sitting out in my backyard under my silver maple tree, bare feet tickled by the cool wet grass beneath me.

Touching the earth with our bare feet connects us in a basic but powerful way to the rest of creation, which, like our own bodies, is a part of God. When we have a tangible link to the ground beneath our feet, it is a reminder of membership in the community of creation. Walking on soft grass, smooth sand, or the cold pebbles of a riverbank reminds us of our animal nature, moving through the landscape in the same way those who wrote the Bible would have done. When we feel our close connection to the land beneath our feet, we are also reminded that we are but one sacred part of an alive wholeness that is the earth.

Chapter 2

THE LAND BELONGS TO GOD

You shall observe my statutes and faithfully keep my ordinances, so that you may live on the land securely. The land will yield its fruit, and you will eat your fill and live on it securely. (Leviticus 25:18–19)

The land shall not be sold in perpetuity, for the land is mine; with me you are but aliens and tenants. Throughout the land that you hold, you shall provide for the redemption of the land. (Leviticus 25: 23–24)

Learning and appreciating the legacy of the land on which we dwell is an integral part of living well on our fragile planet. We are each shaped by our own landscapes and the history of those places. In North America this also involves coming to terms with a long legacy of settler colonialism and violence against Indigenous people. Though such history can make us uncomfortable, it is part of who we are and part of grounding our faith in the earth around us. Another crucial aspect of rooting our faith is learning about the watershed in which we dwell. By developing a more intimate knowledge of our local context, it is easier to step out of our consumer culture mindset and into the beauty of finding God in the present moment.

I was born on the shortgrass prairie of North Texas on what was once the land of the Caddo, the Wichita, and other Indigenous peoples, in a relatively young city called Dallas. The neighborhood where I spent almost my entire childhood had once been a large pecan grove along a creek. When the neighborhood was built, developers left most of the pecan trees intact—nearly every house had at least one in their yard—but paved over the creek. The water couldn't be held underground, though. Persistent springs bubbled up between cracks in the concrete, creating a permanent green mat of algae where water flowed up from the ground and down the street to the storm drain, the remnants of the creek trying to break out.

This landscape shaped who I would become as much as my family and human community did. Every fall my brother and I would collect buckets of pecans from our yard, enough to eat all winter, cracking them under the heels of our shoes and munching on the nuts as we walked to or from school. I was an adult and living in North Carolina before I realized that pecans are quite expensive to buy. They were the free food of my childhood, along with the peaches that dropped from branches that bent over the sidewalk, and the blackberries that grew in the brambly edges between the soccer field and the woods near the school.

At a park just a few miles away, a small patch of the shortgrass prairie that used to stretch across the landscape had been restored, and I used to love wandering around on the paths through the tall grasses and wildflowers. On weekends, when my family ventured out of the city to camp, we saw more of the prairie in the form of ranchland, dotted with cattle, goats, and sheep. The sky was bigger and darker at night, a sea of stars in the dry air. Often, we drove east into the Piney Woods of East Texas, where we were surrounded by hundred-foot-tall pine trees and a cacophony of crickets, frogs, and whippoor-wills at night. As we drove back into Dallas, I began dreaming of the next weekend we'd be able to spend in the woods or on the open plains.

It wasn't until I was an adult that I learned to appreciate the benefits of growing up in the city. The church we attended was full of welcoming, progressive people who, for the most part, accepted difference, cared about social justice, and taught me that thinking critically was not antithetical to faith. I also had access to excellent medical care for my early and complicated disability, and an education in schools where diversity was the norm. I had friends who were black, Muslim, Jewish, Vietnam-ese, and Latino, who opened my eyes to their own beliefs and cultural norms. They challenged any notion that we live in a just society when they faced struggles I did not, because of the color of my skin and the economic privilege of my parents.

Though I have now lived outside of Texas for a longer period than I lived in it, that particular landscape and those people continue to shape my whole being. Something deep within my gut relaxes when the trees finally open out to wide plains somewhere in central Oklahoma, on the drive from Ohio to Texas. My heart feels most at home standing under an oak tree while I look out onto a dry open field of native grasses and wildflowers in gorgeous colors, limestone gravel crunching under my feet.

My faith, too, is intimately bound up with that landscape. As Texan Presbyterians, my family made pilgrimages to Mo Ranch, a Presbyterian camp in the Hill Country outside Kerr-ville, land of sheep ranches and clear spring-fed rivers. I have spent at least one weekend a year there almost every year since I was born. My brother and I swam in the Guadalupe River and worshiped on the top of the tallest hill that looked out on the rest of the county—a land that I always imagined looked very similar to Galilee. When I picture the stories of the gospels, it is this landscape that provides the setting in my mind.

For as much as we like to think of Christianity as a global religion for all people—and it is, in the sense that it is practiced around the world—we often lose sight of the fact that it is only ever local in practice. Just as each of us is shaped by place, so too are our communities of faith. For some reason, though, we often act as though faith and church are or ought to be the same everywhere. We try to force our way of doing things—which are often shaped by our own landscapes and experiences—onto others, who have been shaped by a completely different context. We see our own understanding of the world around us as the standard, forgetting that the Bible was written by people with a dramatically different awareness of this same experience of living on this earth. Coming to terms with our own particular landscapes—including their histories, and the ways they shape us—is crucial in understanding the rootedness of the faith of our ancestors. And only when we do this can we begin to understand and live into the biblical models provided for us of what it might look like to live well on a fragile planet.

THOSE WHO CAME BEFORE

We begin by looking at the history of the land on which we reside. Unless you are an Indigenous person, if you live in North America you are living on land that has been stolen from someone else. This is a hard truth to swallow, but any authentic attempt to root ourselves in our local ecosystem must start

2. The Land Belongs to God

from this uncomfortable awareness. Many Mennonites in my congregation can trace their families' roots in the Midwest back to their arrival in the mid-1800s from Ukraine, Germany, or Switzerland. Their ancestors were some of the first white settlers of Ohio, Indiana, and Illinois, when these lands had just been cleared of their original Indigenous inhabitants by the American government. These refugees from Europe were fleeing religious persecution, and to them the wide-open land here was a godsend, a safe place in which to establish communities and raise families. But just a few years before, this land had been the home of other nations—the Shawnee, the Miami, the Potawatomi, and many others. By the mid-1800s, the last of those inhabitants had been forced from their land, though removal had begun much earlier.

At the heart of this uncomfortable truth is the Doctrine of Discovery, which is an international public law dating to the mid-fifteenth century that declared so-called uninhabited land outside of Europe—meaning land not populated by Christians—as fair game for colonization. European nations, and later the United States, "claimed" land in the Americas, Africa, and Asia for themselves, despite the fact that there were already nations of people living in these places.[1] The Doctrine of Discovery was used to legitimize land claims by the colonizing nations until the 1950s.

In the United States, it was upheld by the Supreme Court multiple times in the nineteenth century to justify the taking of Indigenous lands across the nation. This was done in the name of Jesus—colonizing nations used biblical texts to support their ideology, and until the Protestant Reformation, the pope was the mediator of land claims from competing nations. Christianity is deeply implicated in this legacy of colonization and extermination, a legacy that exemplifies the misuse of religion by white European and American powers to justify their colonizing actions to take the land of people of color.

Ohio, where I now reside, had been populated by a variety of Indigenous nations for around 15,000 years, with the first human inhabitants making their way to the area through the Bering land bridge from Asia. A particularly powerful and organized nation known as the Hopewell people left an enduring mark on the landscape of the Ohio River Valley, building a series of mounds in geometric patterns, including one in the shape of a giant serpent. Before the Revolutionary War, Ohio was home to at least five major Indigenous nations, and the land that is now the city of Columbus was the territory of the Shawnee.

In the early 1800s, settlement by white colonists began to curtail Indigenous control of the lands after a series of battles and treaties. The process culminated in the Indian Removal Act passed by Andrew Jackson in 1830. In 1843, the Wyandot people in the Sandusky region were the last to be relocated to Oklahoma, completely opening Ohio for white settlement.

This is the land on which I, a descendent of white settlers from Germany and Scotland, dwell. A creek near my house is called Bill Moose Run, named after the last Indigenous inhabitant of my neighborhood. He was a member of the Wyandot nation who moved to Columbus after his people's removal and lived along the stream that bears his name for the remainder of his life, dying at the age of one hundred in 1937.[2] Some older inhabitants of the Clintonville neighborhood still remember listening to him tell stories when they were children.

Though the state of Ohio doesn't have any federally recognized tribal reservations, many Indigenous people still live here. NAICCO, the Native American Indian Center of Central Ohio, is one such community, made up of people from various

Indigenous groups who gather to celebrate their heritage and support one another. They currently have a land campaign and are raising money to purchase twenty acres of land in central Ohio, where members will be able to live and hold large community events.

While it's important to learn the history of the Indigenous people in our countries, we must also honor the living, breathing communities of Indigenous people who dwell among us. Though we should be ever wary of the dangers of cultural appropriation, these Indigenous communities contain a wealth of knowledge, and we ought to be listening to what their many voices have to say. Indigenous groups are hardly homogenous, and their beliefs about the animate world as well as human culture are amazingly diverse, but they have in common a deep regard for the land and a wisdom about how to live well within the limits of the land.

As described in the previous chapter, Randy Woodley has characterized this as the Harmony Way, a concept that is part of his Cherokee culture as well as the many other Indigenous cultures whose members he surveyed. The descendants of settlers are relative newcomers to this land, and so it makes sense that we would seek the counsel of those who have dwelled on this continent for tens of thousands of years.

THE LIMITS OF TIME: TOWARD A SPATIAL POINT OF VIEW

Another concept that is common to many Indigenous communities is an emphasis on place rather than an abstract notion of linear time. The Western obsession with time often prevents us from experiencing this kind of connection to particular spaces. Industrialized societies place a premium on the idea of progress and on being busy—these are the engines of our economy. We are taught from a young age that we should always be working, always be moving toward a goal that will improve our situation. Economic activity comes first; it's only the time left over that we can dedicate to friends, family, and ourselves. Those who don't fit into the mold of productivity—most notably people with intellectual and physical disabilities—are seen as a drag on the rest of society, as a hindrance, even as less than human.

This fixation on time and its related notions of constant productivity and social mobility is harmful, because it places people's only value in society in their work, their function, and not in the fullness of their being. In the capitalist system, humans are meant to earn income and spend that income on goods and services. People who don't fit into this model are relegated to secondary status. We define ourselves and each other by how we fit into the economic structure of our society, and advancing our career or social status becomes more important than who we are as whole people and as children of God. By placing a premium on social advancement, we discount the benefit of remaining in one geographic area and putting down roots in a community.

Connected to this idea of productivity and progress is the cultural obsession with either "the good old days" on one end or some utopic future toward which we are moving on the other. The former is the logic inherent in the "Make America Great Again" slogan, which suggests that the United States was great at some prior point in its history, and that the nation has since lost its way. It's no coincidence that those most often adhering to this way of thinking are white men; the past was certainly not great for women or people of color, who were treated like property and had no rights in the early republic.

The idea of progress may be more alluring for many of us. Of course, we want to believe that humanity is moving toward a better future. And some data bears this out. War and overall levels of violence are decreasing globally.[3] Extreme poverty has also decreased dramatically in the last thirty years, while at the same time life expectancy has risen. However, other facts don't paint as pretty a picture.[4] Democracy is under increasing threat, including in the United States, and declines in violence and gains in health are far from universal.[5] Well-being in the United States is still heavily correlated by zip code, meaning that while some people live in relative peace and plenty, others live under constant threat of violence from both the police and gangs.[6]

Ultimately, there seem to be two options: when things seem to be improving or going well, we feel hopeful and optimistic about life. When things appear to be getting worse, we lament the state of the world. These views are connected by their shared positioning of chronological time as the ultimate marker of meaning in our lives—we call this temporal awareness. When we look to cultures that are more grounded in the earth, however, we find another way.

Contrary to an obsession with time, the worldview of most of the planet's Indigenous peoples instead privileges what is called a spatial awareness. They understand their locations as places of continuing revelation, and they live their lives in relation to these places and the community of species within them. In their context, the natural world is a place where the Holy is perpetually being revealed in new ways. Particular places become special because of events that happen there, and when people pass through that place again, they remember the event and the moral lessons that were learned there. In Western culture we tend to rely mostly on texts as our "places of learning," and words are meant to provide moral lessons for all people in all times. This is in contrast to a contextual knowledge that comes from a close relationship with the land and a particular community.

Ecotheologian Jawanza Eric Clark is one of several voices trying to redefine Christian theology in these spatial terms. By this he means "reframing space, and land specifically, as a theological symbol; reconstructing our notion of God; addressing the failure resulting from an overreliance on traditional Christian symbols like the cross and the Bible; and finally reexamining the goal, or telos, of Black liberation theology."[7] He suggests that traditional Christian theology has been overly focused on the historical events of Jesus' birth, death and resurrection, on the idea that a wholly transcendent God broke into history in the form of Jesus Christ, and on the idea that the tenets of Christianity are universal and not culturally specific. This approach to theology focuses Christians either on the past—the time of Jesus—or the future—with the coming end of time, or eschaton.

Part of this conception of God is the notion that God as the Alpha and Omega knows the beginning and end of things, and so guides history to a good end. Clark points out that this is problematic for those experiencing oppression in the here and now, because it presumes that this oppression is the will of God, moving humans toward the right ordering of the world. Such a God is also alienated from the natural world, outside of space and time.[8] With this view, we fail to value and care for the natural world because it is only a backdrop for God's special relationship with humans.

Drawing on his African heritage Clark offers a different possibility: he suggests instead that "a spatial conception of reality demands that we do theology—without being distracted by the distant past or preparing for an unknown future—based on our experience of the natural world in the lived spaces we encounter in every present moment."[9] Challenging the preoccupation with time, Clark asks us to consider what it would mean to center our theology in the present moment and in our own particular places.[10] He turns to African spirituality to draw inspiration for a spatially-oriented theology: "Historically, African-descended people in the Western hemisphere drew from an indigenous African spiritual tradition that expressed a spatially oriented religiosity that places great value on communication with God/the spirits, or discerning divine revelation, in the present moment within the present space(s)."[11] God is not just in the Bible, this theology tells us, but is everywhere in the natural world (similar to the Celtic Christian theology discussed in the previous chapter).

This Africa-based ecotheology leads to concrete action: the reclaiming and restoration of land for the benefit of oppressed people. Rather than striving merely for liberation in the political realm, as has been the concern of much of liberation theology, Clark notes that "spatially oriented telos of liberation manifests land recovery, revitalization, and ecological healing."[12]

There are several prominent examples of this type of land reclamation happening historically and in the present day, including Freedom Farm Cooperative in Sunflower County, Mississippi, founded by Fannie Lou Hamer in the 1970s, and Beulah Land Farms in Calhoun Falls, South Carolina, in the present day.

Beulah Land Farms was started by Albert B. Cleage Jr. and his congregation in Atlanta, the Pan African Orthodox Christian Church, also known as the Shrines of the Black Madonna. Over the course of the 1990s, this church purchased over four thousand acres in rural South Carolina in the face of fierce opposition from white neighbors, banks, and the United States Department of Agriculture.[13] The land use at the farm currently includes cattle ranching, solar farming, agriculture, summer camps, and affordable housing.[14]

Similarly, Soul Fire Farm outside Albany, New York, is "an African/Indigenous centered community farm working to feed people, mostly Black and brown . . . who suffer from food scarcity and live in food-apartheid communities."[15] Other land reclamation projects are planned in both the United States and Liberia.

These are tangible ways that communities are living out a faith that is rooted in the land as well as empowering brown and Black people, who have been most maligned by the prevailing social order. In Clark's words, "something is missing if the contours of liberation are confined solely to various forms of the political economy. . . . What is missing is consideration of the Earth and how liberation must also take into consideration the problem of impending ecocide and the legacy of racist land dispossession. Liberation should not be understood solely within a Eurocentric temporal conception of progress."[16]

An emphasis on place and dwelling well on the land allows us to leave behind these damaging ideas of progress and a preoccupation with history and to include instead those—humans and countless other species—who have been destroyed in the name of such progress.

In addition to such systemic injustice, this fixation on time and productivity perpetuated by the modern industrial culture also takes a significant toll on human emotional well-being. Most notably, in the words of environmental ethicists Whitney Bauman and Kevin O'Brien, in their book *Environmental Ethics and Uncertainty,*

> Chronological time produces anxiety because it places all
> of our thinking into an abstract sense that is literally "out

of this world" and "out of this universe." Time, an abstraction, becomes more important than immediate and present relationships. In a world sped up by fossil fuels, the abstraction of time creates a pace of progress that far outstrips the regenerative capacities of the planet, which evolved at their own pace and have no regard for our abstractions.[17]

This is why we feel so harried in our everyday lives, moving from one task to another, from one meeting to the next, burning all the gas in our cars in the process. Bauman and O'Brien note that many religious traditions offer a space to step outside of this relentless abstraction of chronological time to pay attention to the present moment through ritual practices like liturgical cycles in the Christian year and meditation in Buddhism.[18]

There is one thing these ecotheologians are telling us: time isn't actually real. At least, not in the seconds-minutes-hours structures we've imposed on our experience of living on this earth. Time is a concept created when the first railroads were being built. In the late nineteenth century, the electric clock was invented, and time was standardized in order to organize the burgeoning world of international commerce. Before then, people experienced time through the rhythms of nature—by observing the rising and setting of the sun, and by noticing local seasonal patterns. This is how Jesus understood time, and how the early Christians oriented themselves in relation to time.

While there are certainly merits to chronological time, and it is a needed abstraction for a global world to be able to run, recapturing the biblical understanding of what it means to live well on this planet requires that we remember time remains just that—an abstraction.

WATERSHEDS AND THEIR LIMITS

What does a renewed emphasis on spatial reality, on our particular landscapes, look like from a practical perspective? One answer to this question of deeper rootedness in places is the concept of watershed discipleship.

Ched Myers is one of the leading figures in the watershed discipleship movement, and he notes that the term *watershed discipleship* has a triple meaning. First, humanity is currently in a "watershed historical moment of crisis" that demands environmental engagement from all people.[19] Second, we all live in particular landscapes shaped by their own watersheds, and the life and teachings of Jesus were rooted in his specific bioregional context.[20] Third, we should all be disciples of our particular watersheds, advocating for their well-being and health.[21]

Before we dive in further, it's important to understand what exactly a watershed is. John Wesley Powell, famous explorer and geographer, was the first to provide a modern definition of a watershed, which is "that area of land, a bounded hydrological system, within which all living things are inextricably linked by their common water course and where, as humans settled, simple logic demanded that they become part of the community."[22]

We may not realize it as we go about our days, but our whole lives revolve around water. The human body cannot survive for long at all without it. And water is at once local and global. The water in the cup sitting on the desk next to me came from a nearby reservoir fed by Big Walnut Creek, via a water treatment plant and miles of pipes underneath the ground. But before that, it probably arrived on a cloud from further west, falling as rain. And before that it could have been anywhere in the world. This water will flow through me, nourishing my body, and ultimately end up further down the same river—my house is located in the Olentangy River watershed, a large stream that flows less than a mile east of my house.

Understanding my location in my particular watershed is fairly easy, but the watershed discipleship aspect is slightly more complicated. How can our watershed form us as spiritual beings? Myers notes that the industrial culture of the United States has made most Christians unable to understand the local place they inhabit, noting that "we have been socialized to be more loyal to abstractions and superstructures than literate in the actual biosphere that sustains us; more adept at mobility than grounded in the bioregions in which we reside (but do not truly *inhabit*)."[23] In the industrial West we feel more kinship with our professional sports teams, church denominations, and political parties than we do with our watershed. The watershed provides an alternative identity, a place to ground ourselves in, and become disciples of, a site of ecological restoration in our own backyard.

Why does this matter for us as Christians? The second creation account in Genesis makes it clear that humankind comes from the soil, from the dust of the earth. And our local landscapes are places where God is revealed to us, in the fields and trees and urban streets of our community. Myers argues that "the task of re-placed theology is to reclaim symbols of redemption which are indigenous to the bioregion in which the church dwells, to remember the stories of the peoples of the place, and to sing anew the old songs of the land."[24]

The bioregional focus of watershed discipleship does have its limits. Those of us living in industrialized societies are enmeshed in hundreds, if not thousands, of global supply chains. Unless we are fairly wealthy, most of us must make choices about how to spend our money—choices that often put competing values in conflict. Should I pay more for local fruits and vegetables at the farmers market, or should I pay more for clothing that was made in my own country? Decisions about consumption are always complicated and fraught, and depending on where you live, local produce or clothing might not even be available. Some people have chosen to "purify" their lives, to live entirely off the grid, not dependent on global markets. Their choices are certainly admirable, but they aren't attainable for most people. And an emphasis on living a purely bioregional life can easily degenerate into judging those who are unable to live this way.

An emphasis on the local can also lead to a provincialism that fails to take into account the effects of systemic racism and economic inequality that are pervasive throughout the world. Watershed discipleship assumes that communities will come together to protect their own natural assets, but this is predicated on having a community of people with social equality and equitable distribution of wealth. This kind of equality is certainly a worthy goal to work toward, but in most communities in North America, there is a large gap between those with means and those without. Additionally, it is often those with the most privilege making the decisions about resource use for the rest of the community.

The deeper we dig, the more we see that everything is bound up together with everything else. Racism is deeply intertwined with environmental degradation. Climate change is inextricably connected to wealth inequality and the legacy of settler colonialism globally. We hold two truths in juxtaposition: that it is impossible to tangibly care for the whole world at once, while at the same time every place is bound together with every other place. The local is always where we dwell and where we work toward positive change, but we must also remember the webs we inhabit are vast and sticky, and no one is innocent of the damage inflicted on the earth.

If you take away one thing from this chapter, I hope it is the message that land is important. White settlers have a legacy of taking land from others and claiming it as their own. Indigenous and Black empowerment is centered on reclaiming and renewing land, on having a space in which to rebuild communities. Our particular landscapes matter—each bioregion and watershed—and we ought to protect them as we protect our children. But we equally need to recognize that every watershed on earth deserves protection, and bioregionalism can so easily deteriorate into an attitude of "not-in-my-backyard," a pushing of polluting industries into marginalized communities.

A focus on the well-being of our own land is fruitless if all we do is foist our pollution onto someone else. Living well on our fragile planet entails taking care of our own land, recognizing the history of that land, and ensuring that our actions do not imperil the lands of others. The Bible emphasizes that God dwells in all of creation. So, the best way to gain a greater awareness of God's presence in the world is to become native to our places, to paraphrase the words of Wes Jackson.[25] We can root our faith in the earth by locating ourselves in our particular watershed and seeking out the wisdom of those who have dwelled here before, as we learn to become good tenants of our land.

PUTTING IT INTO PRACTICE: ON WHOSE LAND DO YOU DWELL?
In this chapter I have been concerned mostly with shaking up our inherited industrial focus on time, progress, and productivity at the expense of certain groups of people as well as the natural world. There is a lot to digest as we rethink our

role in this legacy of land dispossession and ecological destruction, either as the oppressors or the oppressed. But there are also plenty of tangible things we can do right now to start to become more rooted in our own places. These include finding out more about the original inhabitants of land you live on, writing a land acknowledgment for your congregation or family, learning about your local watershed, and considering monetary reparations to historically oppressed groups, as part of your church's work in the larger community.

As I mentioned earlier, I live on land that once belonged to the Shawnee nation, and many others before them. In gatherings within my Mennonite regional conference, we often introduce ourselves by also stating whose land we are currently residing on. An excellent resource for finding out about the Indigenous peoples who inhabit(ed) your location is Native Land Digital at https://native-land.ca, which has a map of the entire world overlaid with various nations and tribal entities. There are links to follow for each Indigenous group, where you can learn more about them, often from the tribe or nation themselves.

Closely related to this is the writing or recitation of a land acknowledgement. Land acknowledgments are becoming more prevalent in churches and universities in North America as we begin to deal with our shared legacy of land dispossession. The Native Governance Center[26] and Northwestern University[27] both have excellent resources for writing a land acknowledgment. The Governance Center notes, "It is important to understand the longstanding history that has brought you to reside on the land, and to seek to understand your place within that history. Land acknowledgements do not exist in a past tense, or historical context: colonialism is a current ongoing process, and we need to build our mindfulness of our present participation."[28] Creating a land acknowledgment is meant to be a process of self-reflection as we dig into our own history in a particular place and as we learn how that place has been shaped by the many others who came before us.

An additional practice that churches are beginning to recognize is the payment of monetary reparations to Indigenous and other marginalized groups. This is a new idea that is only beginning to gain greater visibility. The basic idea is that a church would donate all or a portion of the amount that they would pay in property taxes, but don't because of their tax-exempt status, to organizations that are managed by and benefit Indigenous or other marginalized groups. This action is not charity and comes with no strings attached.

As part of my congregation's ongoing commitment to reparative justice, Columbus Mennonite Church pays reparations to NAICCO and an African-American mutual aid fund. This money is not a donation or a gift; it is what we feel is due to our neighbors as reparations for past harms, similar to a voluntary tax. Though we did not personally cause these harms, our church has benefitted, as a majority-white congregation, from the legacy of slavery and Indigenous land dispossession, so part of our money should rightly be returned to those disenfranchised by this economic system of power.

A last practice is finding out about your own local watershed, specifically about where your drinking water comes from and where it goes after you use it, if your house is supplied by a municipality. For locations in the United States the Environmental Protection Agency has an excellent resource called "How's My Waterway?" where you can find all the details of your local watershed, including water quality and who holds permits to discharge into the waterway.[29] To learn more about watersheds in Canada, you can check out https://watersheds .ca. Many municipalities also maintain their own watershed databases, where residents can get information about where their water comes from and is discharged.

If you live in an area prone to flash flooding, planting a rain garden can be a beneficial way to slow the flow of water from your property into the water system. Our neighborhood recently installed rain gardens along some of the steeper streets where rainwater runoff is extreme during storms. The plants and ditches allow water to percolate back into the ground, preventing the sewage lines from overflowing during storms and overburdening the Olentangy River. Our church has had a rain garden in front of the offices for a number of years, an example of what Myers calls "demonstration project evangelism," showing the community how to better care for its local watershed.[30]

Chapter 3

A WILD AND ANIMATE EARTH

But ask the animals, and they will teach you;
the birds of the air, and they will tell you;
ask the plants of the earth, and they will teach you;
and the fish of the sea will declare to you.
Who among all these does not know
that the hand of the LORD has done this?
In his hand is the life of every living thing
and the breath of every human being. (Job 12:7–10)

This beautiful scripture passage evokes a fundamental element of the biblical worldview—that creation contains the
wisdom of God. And yet, how often do we ask birds, fish, or
trees for advice about how to live? Jesus often used this same
kind of language, encouraging his listeners to be like lilies of
the field or sparrows, trusting in the bounty of God found in
the natural world.

But many people face an even more basic problem when it
comes to connecting with the particular living beings of our
ecosystem—we don't even know what they are. How many
species of birds can you recognize on sight? What about trees
or wildflowers? I was in college before I learned the difference

between a red oak and a live oak, which reflects the low status our education system places on knowing the creatures of our local habitats. Learning the names of the plants and animals that share our landscape is an excellent step in connecting to the earth and to the Creator. This knowledge helps us to live well on this fragile planet, because it's hard to care about plants and animals when we don't know anything about them.

I was having lunch with a friend who had recently returned to the United States after living in Chiang Mai, Thailand, for the past five years. When you go for a walk with a Thai person, he told me, you should not expect to get any exercise, because that person will stop you every few steps to tell you about the medicinal qualities of a specific plant growing up out of the sidewalk or about what fruit will be falling from such and such a tree in a few months' time. He was impressed that his Thai friends all know about each plant: what is good to eat, what is helpful for a stomachache or a cold. And he lamented that he knew very few of the plants growing around his house in the United States, or if they are beneficial for anything except curb appeal.

I had another friend in college who got interested in botany after learning that most young people can recognize over 200 brand logos but can recognize fewer than a dozen plants on sight. She wanted to be able to identify just as many plants as brand logos, so she set about learning about the plants she shared her bioregion with.

Sound familiar? This is what I mean when I express frustration about our overall lack of connection with the specifics of the landscapes around us. We are more versed in the culture of consumerism than we are in the plant and animal life that surrounds us. Learning to be part of one's bioregion means getting to know one's nonhuman neighbors and to recognize how our bodies are shaped by the land we inhabit. In addition, living faithfully on a fragile planet entails reconnecting with the sense of aliveness found in both the Bible and in the lives of the biblical writers. It's important to find ways to root ourselves more deeply in the joy and wonder of the natural world, including learning more about the bioregions where we dwell and understanding the landscape in which the Bible was written.

THE BIOREGION OF ANCIENT ISRAEL

To truly understand the words written in the Bible, it's important to know something about the earthy context in which the biblical authors worked. Ancient Israel was at the western edge of the Fertile Crescent, a massive land area that extends from Egypt to the Persian Gulf. The Fertile Crescent got its name because the land within it produced large amounts of grain, enough to feed people and livestock alike in abundance.[1] This resulted in hunter-gatherer bands settling down to become farmers, thus making possible the first empires.

Another key feature of the land of ancient Israel (called Palestine in Roman times) was that it served as a narrow bridge between three continents. Europe, Africa, and Asia all meet in the Fertile Crescent, and that fairly flat stretch of land was a superhighway of sorts for early empires.[2] The empire that controlled the land of Israel was able to exert enormous influence over trade routes, making it an early target for conquering.

The land of the Bible contains three different geographic zones—the coastal plain along the Mediterranean Sea, the mountainous interior, and the Jordan River Valley.[3] The coastal plain is flat and easy to farm, but it was a prime invasion spot because of its location next to the Mediterranean and because its level ground made for easy travel. The central mountains of Israel contain the Galilee region, where Jesus was born and where many of the stories in the Old Testament took place.[4] The mountains are steep and the land is arid, making farming a precarious endeavor. The Jordan River Valley includes the Sea of Galilee and the Dead Sea, connected by the Jordan River. This region is hot because much of it is below sea level, and fishing would have been the main economic activity, with farming on the higher plains.[5]

The most important feature of ancient Israel's landscape was the relative scarcity of water. Israel had one major freshwater lake and a few streams, and for five months of the year there was no rain at all.[6]

In biblical times, water was carefully conserved, stored in cisterns, and pulled from wells. When God promised in Isaiah 58:11 that the people "shall be like a watered garden, like a spring of water, whose waters never fail" if they uphold justice, this would have meant something tangible to those hearing it. The promise of adequate water in parched places was life itself. To be a watered garden or a spring was to be a source of a precious resource, scarce and sacred.

It was in these fragile, gorgeous, rocky ecosystems where the ancient people composed the Bible so many years ago. It was a land that yielded fruit and sustenance only with careful management and skilled use of limited resources, the most scarce of which was water. The Israelites were concerned with how the land would sustain them, but there is lots of evidence that God also cherished the wild plants and animals that had nothing to do with sustaining human life.

A WILD AND ANIMATE EARTH: THE PSALMS AND JOB

In the wisdom literature of the Hebrew Bible, epic poetry depicts the earth in great detail as resplendent and full of life.

It is in the Psalms and Job, some of the oldest writings in the Bible, that the universe unfurls in its animate, wild glory. For example, in Psalm 96:11–12, the earth is depicted as a sentient being that praises God: "Let the heavens be glad, and let the earth rejoice; let the sea roar, and all that fills it; let the field exult, and everything in it. Then shall all the trees of the forest sing for joy."

The heavens and earth participate in the praising of God. The sea and the field are no mere backdrops, but feeling beings that actively participate in the life of the created order. Just a few verses later in Psalm 97:1, the psalmist proclaims, "Let the earth rejoice; let the many coastlands be glad!"

In Psalm 19:1–2 the cosmos actually speaks, presumably imparting wisdom for all to hear, including humans: "The heavens are telling the glory of God; and the firmament proclaims his handiwork. Day to day pours forth speech, and night to night declares knowledge."

How often do we listen to the voice of the sky, the voice of the day and night? And what would this look like? I mark the seasons of my midwestern American landscape with sound. From the silent depths of winter, the birds start calling out to one another in early spring, just as the snowdrops and crocuses begin to burst up from the frozen dark earth. Their song reaches a crescendo in late spring, especially at dawn and dusk. In early May the spring peeper frogs sing in small ponds and along the intermittent stream near my house, if we've had plenty of spring rain. In mid-June the fireflies start to light up the night, silently, their bodies pulsing with light, a slow-motion fireworks show each evening at the edge of the forest. In early July, the cicadas start droning, a hypnotic thrum, like a choir of monks singing, announcing the heat of the day. By August, the cicada chants have been mostly supplanted by the softer hum of crickets, heralding the coming of fall. They keep up their refrain all the way until the first frost in mid-October lays the whole landscape silent once more, except the occasional caw of the crow from the highest branches of the silver maple.

This is the voice of the day and the voice of the night, a soundscape punctuated with life as the days grow longer, then shorter, and fall capitulates to the quiet depths of winter. To reduce all of this life to mere processes of evolution or mechanism is to miss out on the animate vibrancy that surrounds us. It is this kind of speech and praise that the Psalms speak of. Psalm 104 has been held up in particular as an example of creation-oriented liturgy. It is an extended song of praise about the glory of God as manifested in creation. "You stretch out the heavens like a tent," the psalmist says in verse 2, and in verse 4, "You make the winds your messengers, fire and flame your ministers." This psalm makes clear that God is the underlying force of the whole universe, making springs gush forth, planting the trees on the mountainsides, setting the moon and the sun in the sky to mark the day and night.

Enolyne Lyngdoh, an Indian theologian and member of the Khasi community, one of the Indigenous groups of northeast India, interprets this psalm from an Indigenous perspective. She argues that the "poetic praise of God's creation in Psalm 104 portrays intricate inter-connectedness and subtle interdependence of air, soil, water, plants, animals, and human beings," which is incredibly resonant with the Khasi Indigenous worldview.[7] Though this notion of interdependence and the sacredness of the natural world is present in Jewish tradition, it has often been downplayed in theological interpretations of Psalm 104, which have emphasized only God's sovereignty over creation.[8] Lyngdoh notes that this indwelling of God in nature is similar to traditional Khasi beliefs that recognize nature as a manifestation of the sacred, and so Psalm 104 has great resonance with Khasi Christians.

The whirlwind speeches in Job are yet another example of the wild and animate nature of creation in Scripture. Near the end of the book of Job, after Job has spent countless verses pleading for God to intervene in his wreck of a life and asking why he has been subjected to such suffering, God answers him at length from a whirlwind (chapters 38–41). These are some of my favorite passages in the Bible because they depict a creation that is wild, alive, and not made for the benefit of humans. God begins by asking where Job was when the foundations of the earth were laid (Job 38:4). Chapter 38 is an entire recounting of the creation and ordering of the heavens and the earth: stars, oceans, clouds, rains, day, and night. Chapter 39 is a detailed account of the lives and value of the wild animals, which have no relationship with humans and live entirely outside the sphere of human influence. The message is clear—there is much more to the earth than human life. Instead, the lives of wild ox, lions, mountain goats, deer, and hawks are at the forefront. In chapters 40 and 41, God discusses the lives of two giant creatures, Behemoth and Leviathan, who are clearly meant to be the top predators of the earth, free and wild and strong.

The book of Job is a reminder that we are infinitesimally small in the cosmic scale of life, and that God is not bound by human notions of justice and moral order. God, and the universe, are infinitely vaster than we can even begin to imagine. The whirlwind speeches are also an ode to the chaotic elements of the natural world, that which is beyond the control of humans. We come before thunderstorms in awe, and we know little about the intricate workings of wild ecosystems in uninhabitable mountains and deserts. These natural elements remind us that plenty happens that is valuable to God, outside the scope of human culture.

AN EARTHBOUND SAVIOR: JESUS AS SHAMAN HEALER

The gospels are full of earthy, rooted stories and parables from Jesus' life and ministry. They demonstrate that God cares about the plants and animals of the earth just as much as humans—the lilies of the field, sparrows, and more. As discussed in chapter 1, Jesus' descriptions of the kingdom of God often included agricultural metaphors, language the rural Israelites would have been familiar with and which are easily lost on modern urban humans. But Jesus' teachings reflect more than the pastoral landscape around him. He was also on a mission to subvert the social order imposed by the Roman authorities and upheld by the local religious establishment. He turned over tables in the Temple and questioned the power of the empire. Even more than that, Jesus was a healer, and the Gospels are full of healing stories, recounting ways in which he radically transformed both the lives of individuals in the lowest levels of society and those in authority.

It is not difficult to recognize Jesus as a philosopher, teacher, and political reformer, but we often forget how common healing miracle stories are in the Gospels. Jesus was not only teaching and gathering followers; he was also healing people, often with natural elements.[9] We might be uncomfortable with healing stories because they offend our modern sensibilities about how medicine and disease function, and also because these sorts of miracles do not seem to be happening in the world today. Faith healing is often seen as a charlatan act, an attempt to squeeze money out of the poor and desperate, and it sometimes is. Sadly, there are those who prey upon the pain and hope of others. But this is not the same as Jesus' healing.

As someone with a disability, I feel uncomfortable with the miracle stories, because I don't maintain any hope that Jesus or anyone else is going to heal me of my permanent disability. And we certainly are not promised this kind of healing. It's easy to gloss over the fact that healing stories make up a lot of Jesus' work in the gospels—casting out demons, restoring sight, healing chronic bleeding—because we don't know what to do with the miraculous or what it means for us today.

Religion scholar Mark Wallace, in *When God Was a Bird*, argues that these healing stories demonstrate Jesus' power as a healer or shaman, intervening in people's lives, often those at the bottom of the social hierarchy. To enact his healing, Jesus used natural elements—dirt, plant oils, animals, spring water, even his own spit—combining them with the supernatural power of the Creator. In the gospel of John, chapter 9, Jesus healed a blind man by making a paste out of his spit and the dirt and putting it in the man's eyes. These are like earthy holy elements, complementary to the wine and bread of the Eucharist.[10] Jesus was also able to channel the natural elements, calming storms and feeding the crowds of followers that came to hear him preach. In Wallace's words, "Living in the lap of creation's many gifts, Jesus harnesses the curative powers of the earth to do something radical and unexpected within his community."[11]

These shamanistic abilities to heal and calm storms were an outgrowth of Jesus' close relationship with the landscape around him and his connection with the power of the Creator. Wallace wrote, "Jesus' shamanism, his ability to channel divine power through the natural world—grew out of his founding encounters with Spirit-filled landscapes and creatures in their everyday habitats."[12] Jesus was a homeless wanderer, spending most of his time outside, and retreating to mountainous wild habitats to restore his soul. During his last night, just before his arrest, he camped on the Mount of Olives, a particularly sacred place, and sought comfort in the garden there (Luke 22:39–46).

Jesus' healing is fully intertwined with his teachings—both seek to restore shalom and point people toward what it means to live well, particularly uplifting those who are marginalized in society. Theologian James Perkinson argues that, in his teachings, Jesus sought to upend the empire with a return to a gift economy, where goods are shared equally among people. Perkinson writes, "His own movement practice does not so much seek to gain entry into imperial 'prosperity' (that is, imperial plunder) for the poor, as to return people to the land and to each other, in trust that the soil will produce 'of itself' (Mark 4:28) and the rain and sun and seed and seasons do their work as divine gift (Matt 5:45, Mark 4:1–9:29)."[13] Jesus promised living water (John 7:37–38), repudiating the privatization of water by the Roman Empire.[14]

This sharing in order to meet basic needs is evident in numerous parables as well as in the invocation for daily bread in the Lord's Prayer. And there is evidence that this lifestyle of sharing of goods was adopted in the early Christian communities. Acts 2:44–45 notes, "All who believed were together and had all things in common; they would sell their possessions and goods and distribute the proceeds to all, as any had need." This is as strong a repudiation of capitalism as there is, that these early followers of Jesus gave up everything that was theirs for the good of the community. Not many of us can say that we would do the same, deeply enmeshed as we are in today's culture of capitalism.

Jesus' life, and the lives of his early followers, are difficult to emulate. Few of us even come close to giving up all we have in order to serve God, except perhaps those in monastic orders. That's not the only point of the Gospels, though. What appeals most to me about Jesus' words and actions is the continual invitation to participate in a different mode of being, to worry less about material comfort and more about how one's actions help foster the kin-dom of heaven on earth. I want to live my life in a way that is not wantonly destructive of other life, human and nonhuman. Perhaps this is what it means to live into the healing stories of Jesus in my own life, to refrain from causing harm to others and working for healing where I can. Because I live in a developed country that gets most of its resources and goods from poorer countries, this is a tall order. But this is the vision to which the Gospels call us.

FINDING GOD IN OUR OWN BIOREGION: CULTIVATING WONDER

Although the Bible was written in the context of a dry landscape for mostly mountain- and desert-dwelling people, its words have powerful things to say to us, even though we live in a vastly different time and across various types of landscapes. Though it may not always be at the forefront of our minds, water is precious to us—sacred even—as a source of life, just as it was to them. And when the psalmist and the writer of Job evoke the aliveness of a wild creation, they were making a statement about the fundamental nature of reality and the role of humans in it. We are at once tiny, insignificant creatures in a vast universe as well as people chosen by God.

The best place to start when trying to reconnect with the vibrant aliveness of creation depicted in the Bible is to step outside and experience our own landscapes more deeply. In order to do this, we have to reorient ourselves away from a mechanistic view of nature as a mindless machine and toward a recognition that the world is a "living field, an open and dynamic landscape" in which our lives and the earth's life are intricately woven together, in the words of David Abram.[15]

This notion of the world as a living field in which we participate is the opposite of the dualistic worldview first posited by René Descartes in the seventeenth century, exemplified by his famous phrase, "I think, therefore I am." This simple statement positions humans as the only thinking beings in the universe, equating all other creatures to simple automatons existing entirely without thought or creativity. It also suggests that humans are able to objectively view reality from the outside, as if we are brains walking around making observations in a world of which we are not a part. But the truth is that it's impossible to be an objective viewer, because our very animal presence in the world changes whatever we view, including ourselves. Humans are embedded in the web of the cosmos, inseparable from our embodied existence. We aren't simply minds walking around inhabiting bodies; mind and body are two aspects of our cohesive whole.

Bodies are important in all of this, as being aware of our physical reality opens us up to the present moment. As one of earth's animals, the human being is inextricably linked in webs of relationships with other beings, and true perception is the awareness of this reciprocity between organisms. Abram describes this as "a sort of silent conversation that I carry on with things, a continuous dialogue that unfolds far below my verbal awareness. . . . Whenever I quiet the persistent chatter of words within my head, I find this silent or wordless dance always already going on—this improvised duet between my animal body and the fluid, breathing landscape that it inhabits."[16] People once used to read the landscape in the same way we now read books, looking for game trails in the brush, or discerning upcoming weather from cloud formations. We were intimately connected with the animate natural processes, and our ability to read the language of the land was directly related to our ability to thrive in our ecological environment. Abram argues that our ability to make stories springs to life in our minds because what we read is an outgrowth of our imaginative and receptive engagement with the landscape. He posits that written language has subsumed the original language of the animate earth.

Learning to speak this original language is an important aspect of being present in the current moment and appreciating the aliveness of creation. But it can be hard to actually pay attention to the present moment. So many things vie for our attention: bills to pay, errands to run, tasks to finish at work, groceries to buy. We are almost always at the mercy of an internal dialogue, overthinking past events, fretting about the future, and we spend little time being present where we are.

Abram describes an exercise he sometimes does "to keep myself from falling completely into the oblivion of linear time": He goes to an open outdoor space and centers his mind with a few deep breaths. Then he closes his eyes and imagines his future and his past "as two vast balloons of time, separated from each other like the bulbs of an hourglass, yet linked together at the single moment where I stand pondering them." Then he visualizes these large balloons leaking into the present moment, the slender center of the hourglass, which begins to grow larger and larger, while the future and past become "mere knots" on the edge of this immense center.

This experience makes him feel as if he is "standing in the midst of an eternity, a vast and inexhaustible present. The whole world rests within itself."[17] This exercise helps Abram reclaim a sense of the spacious present in which we humans always dwell but are rarely conscious of in our fixation on the past and our anxiety about the future.

It is clear that we modern humans have cut ourselves off from the rhythms of the natural world. To be whole, to be fully ourselves again, we must reclaim those rhythms. We have fallen in love with the self-focused rewards of consumer culture to the detriment of the earth and our relationship with the creating God. As we have seen, the Bible shows that, to God and to Jesus, bodies matter—the well-being and flourishing of physical bodies. A human being is not just a disembodied immortal soul.

Another way we pursue this flourishing of our bodies is by cultivating wonder for the natural world around us as God's magnificent creation. Another environmental philosopher, Andreas Weber, uses the term *eros*—the Greek word for love—to capture this sense of wonder and connection we can find when we immerse ourselves in the natural world and strengthen our relationships with the rest of those bound up in the web of life with us. Eros can also mean a deep sense of sharing, communication, and creative connection with others, including the natural world.[18] In this sense, love is an ecological process, because it provides a framework for describing these dense webs of relationship. Weber writes:

> To understand love, we must understand life. To be able to love, as subjects with feeling bodies, we must be able to be alive. To be allowed to be fully alive is to be loved. To allow oneself to be fully enlivened is to love oneself—and at the same time, to love the creative world, which is principally and profoundly alive. This is the fundamental thesis of erotic ecology.[19]

This connection between love and life is foundational to how I understand the love of God. The Creator instilled her love in all of the cosmos—trillions of living beings, all bound up with one another. Life suffuses our planet and so also does love. Love is the energy of connection that links all things. So, when we say that God is love, it is these infinite connections that come to my mind.

THE BUILDING BLOCKS OF A LANDSCAPE

Cultivating wonder and awakening to the loving connection that pulses through the world is all well and good, but it's hard to love what you don't know. This is why it is so crucial to learn about the actual creatures we share our landscapes with. Whenever I travel somewhere new, I always try to learn about the landscape where I'm going. It helps me feel more at home wherever I am and live better—more fully—on this fragile planet.

Without delving headlong into the ecological sciences (though there's plenty of richness there if you'd like to dive deeper!), you will find four basic aspects of the landscape that are helpful for understanding the more than human world: the physical ground beneath your feet, the plants that grow in your bioregion, the animals that live around you, and the climate that shapes all life in your area. Gaining even this basic level of knowledge will help you orient yourself in your corner of creation.

First, it's helpful to start with the ground you're standing on, literally. The substrate of my Texas childhood was bright white limestone with a thin layer of rich black soil on top. Here in Ohio, I dwell on a bedrock of Ohio shale beneath several yards of clay-like earth. When we pay attention to the ground, we're participating in geology—the study of the earth's physical surface, both its structures and its history. The rocks beneath our feet hold the entire history of our planet, our deep past. If you want a gorgeous introduction to geology, check out the website of an organization called USGS, where you will find an intricate geologic map of North America.[20] Knowing about local rocks might not seem as important as learning about plants and animals, but these geologic formations are the foundation layer of the landscape, the land that makes all other life possible.

When the psalmist writes that the rocks and hills will cry out, it is the sense of deep history and the ground of our being that they speak to, as well as these rocky structures beneath our feet, which are also animate beings. Some kinds of stone hold a living record of the ancient history of earth. Limestone, in particular, holds fossilized sea creatures—snails and clams, fish, even aquatic plants—remnants from when much of the earth was covered with a shallow, warm ocean. We also think of the earth beneath us when we consider more recent history, because the ground is where we bury the dead, returning human bodies to the earth from which they came. All living organisms eventually return to the soil, which gestates life, the ultimate regenerator.

Second, we can learn about the plants that are all around us, enveloping us in every bioregion, in amazing variety. Plant life is present on almost every surface of the earth where the warm rays of the sun reach. Humans and animals depend on plants for sustenance, both directly and indirectly. Plants are some of the oldest life-forms on the planet, stretching all the way back to the red algae that was present in India 1.6 billion years ago.[21] Some are also incredibly long-lived. The oldest known living tree is a bristlecone pine in the Great Basin of California, a tree that has been dated to be over 5,000 years old, older than the Roman Empire.[22] Learning to identify the plants in your yard or neighborhood is one of the best ways to begin to connect with the landscape around you.

I became interested in botany—the study of plants—when I was in college. I found myself in an entirely different part of the country surrounded by all these plants I didn't recognize. Learning their names was a way of claiming the steep green mountains of western North Carolina as my home. When I walked through the forest, I began to recognize familiar plants that became like friends—bloodroot, indian cucumber, and jack-in-the-pulpit on the forest floor, with tall shagbark hickory, red oak, and red maple towering over me. On steep hillsides I encountered thick mazes of rhododendron and fir trees at higher elevations. Each new plant name that I learned became another link in the chain that connected me to that place. When I was anxious, I would recite their Latin names as I walked—like tangible prayers that rooted me to this specific part of the earth—and I felt calmed.

Back when I was learning to identify plants, I carried around several heavy guidebooks in my backpack. Today, the same plant keys and descriptions are available in an abundance of mobile phone apps. There are even apps that use your camera to match the plant you are seeing to a database in order to identify it. Free apps like Pl@nt Net and iNaturalist give basic facts about any plants you might see, and iNaturalist even lets you share your findings with other app users. If you enjoy the heft and ease of a real book like I do, *Newcomb's Wildflower Guide* and the National Audubon Society's *Field Guide to Trees* are two of my favorites.

Third, we can learn about the animals that share in our curious life, moving among us even when we do not see them. The animal kingdom includes a vast array of different creatures, from insects and fish to birds and large carnivores. Animals are our brothers and sisters in the landscape and can be found even in the most urban of environments. Many animals have adapted to cohabitate near humans—including deer, coyotes, foxes, rabbits, and pigeons. Depending on what bioregion you inhabit, you might see or hear bobcats, black or brown bears, pelicans, dolphins, or mountain lions.

Deer are a daily sight in my yard. All last summer and fall, my stretch of the neighborhood hosted a doe and her two fawns. We got to know one another quite well, and when I was sitting in the yard, she would often graze warily nearby.

If you live in a part of the country where snow falls, winter can be an excellent time to figure out who is crossing your landscape. I often hear coyotes howling in the late afternoon and evening in the forest behind the house, but I have never seen one. After a recent snow, however, I saw clear coyote tracks in the snow, near the perimeter of the fence, along with tracks of rabbits, squirrels, and the ever-present deer. It appears that our yard is something of an animal superhighway. After the same snow, I was at a nature reserve down by a pond and saw muskrat tracks along the boardwalk.

Consider looking for an animal track guide and carrying it with you when you're outside. It's amazing how many animals leave their footprints in mud, snow, and sand, even the ones you may never set eyes on.

When you do catch a glimpse of something rare or shy, it can be a profound spiritual experience. The first time I saw wolves in the wild, I was completely awestruck. I was at Denali National Park and Preserve on a trip with my mother and my aunt, and we were taking a bus tour through the park, the only way to get into the park except on foot. Late in the day, we were driving down the road, returning to the lodge after observing herds of caribou and taking in wild, scenic vistas of the tundra landscape. My feet were cold, and my knees were sore from sitting all day in the cramped seat of the repurposed yellow school bus. Then, suddenly, we came upon the loping figure of a lone gray wolf trotting along the grass verge of the gravel road ahead of us. We passed by slowly, and the beautiful animal kept up its steady gait, another traveler on the road. I was most struck by how different she felt to me than the captive wolves at the zoo. She emanated a feeling of freedom and contentment that I cannot describe. She belonged deeply to this vast landscape. I was only a temporary resident passing through.

When we are able to observe animals in the wild, we learn something about God and ourselves. We learn that the world is so much bigger than our human minds can imagine and that there is wholeness in the world that doesn't involve us. I think this is what the writer of Job was trying to say in the speeches of God from the whirlwind. Creation is vast and infinitely diverse, and for all that we have settled, there are still large swaths of wilderness where humans have scarcely set foot—the Siberian tundra, the Northwest Territories of Canada, the dense rainforests in the heart of the Amazon. Unfortunately, because of climate change, our actions are impacting life even in these remotest regions of the planet, which leads us to the last element—weather.

The climate—of which the weather is one aspect—is the primary force (along with latitude) that determines what living things dwell around us. Weather is also something of a basic language we humans share with one another—over small talk in the grocery store or with our neighbors. We comment on the recent rain, or how wonderful it is to see the sun, or we wonder when the heat wave will finally let up. Talking about the weather is a way of connecting with other people in a way that also grounds us in a shared reality. For those of us who live in a temperate climate, the seasons are the constant refrain of our lives. The brittle cold of winter slowly melts into spring, in a cacophony of colorful flowers, and the rich green abundance of summer fades slowly into the quiet oranges and reds of fall colors, with leaves that the cold rain and wind pull off the trees, settling us into winter once more. For people in hotter parts of the world, the seasonal change is characterized by the presence or absence of rain, dividing life into the rainy season and the dry season.

Climate also includes the air around us, full of heady scents and messages from plants and animals alike. We usually think of the air as a void, empty space in front of our faces, but the air is more full of life than we can imagine. It envelops us in the soft humidity of a summer morning or wakes us up with the fierce polar wind. Plants and animals emit pheromones into the air to communicate with others of their kind, signaling danger or a nearby pest. Humans share the ability to breathe with almost all organisms on earth, and breath and spirit are closely related concepts.

The Greek word for spirit, *pneuma*, is the same as that for breath, and means literally "air in motion."[23] The four Hebrew letters that denote the name of God in the Old Testament, YHVH, when spoken aloud, sound like breathing. If to have a soul means to breathe, we are in much larger company than traditional Western theology would have us believe.

You probably already have all the resources you need to understand your particular climate; you may have an entire lifetime of experience in that region. But the world is experiencing an increasingly unpredictable climate, with unprecedented droughts, floods, wildfires, and hurricanes happening on a regular basis. The air around us is changing. I've only been on this planet for forty years, but even in my lifespan I have recognized changes. Snowstorms have become much less frequent, and hot days linger later and later in the year.

One way to connect with your climate over a span of years is to keep a weather diary, recording snowfalls, rainstorms, the first and last freezing days. Some people also record when certain species of birds appear in their yard and when flowers bloom. Writing down these small bits of information year after year can help you connect more deeply to the rhythms of the seasons in your particular place and help you learn to live a more richly interconnected life on this fragile planet.

WAKING UP TO OUR WILD AND ANIMATE EARTH

There is so much life that surrounds us in our particular landscapes, and it is easy to live in awe—if we only remember to wake up and pay attention. When Job implores his friends to ask the birds and the animals for knowledge of God, he is saying something fundamental about both the Creator and creation. God's presence is suffused in everything around us—rocks, sky, moss, and cardinals. To understand the mindset of those who crafted the Bible and the mindset of Jesus, we must also bind ourselves more deeply to the natural world. This includes the awareness that creation is made up of living, feeling organisms that have their own language. We can be alert to hear them.

Jesus also encouraged his followers to live as part of the gift economy of nature, reminding them that all they need comes from the living beings around them and that hoarding the bounty of creation is a sin against God. Though we in the modern culture are hopelessly tangled in systems of capitalist exploitation, we can still take steps to recognize our enmeshment in a much more holistic web of life, and we can minimize our impact on the earth and its many human and nonhuman communities. It begins by paying attention to the ecosystems of our own landscapes, orienting ourselves in our current places.

PUTTING IT INTO PRACTICE: NATURE WALK

The best way to begin to connect with your own landscape is simple: walk outside and pay attention. By going on a nature walk, either in your neighborhood or a nearby park, you can deepen your awareness of the land around you and all its inhabitants. You can go on a nature walk with a group or individually; the important thing is to go slowly and pay attention to everything around you.

The nature walks that are organized by my congregation's creation care group are always intentional about setting the tone. We begin with a short reading related to nature and then we have a centering prayer before we start walking. The leader reminds us that this is a time for quiet and patient observation, not for idle talking or walking quickly. We often will cover only a single mile in a two-hour span of time, but the experience is well worth it.

Here are some ideas for how to do a nature walk:

1. Choose a time and a place where you will be able to observe nature without too much interference from crowds or loud noises.
2. Set the intention. Read a scripture passage, a poem, or a quote from a naturalist to start off the time. Use it as a reminder that this is a sacred time for listening to the natural world. Before starting out, say a prayer or have a period of silent contemplation.

3. Move slowly. It may be hard to simply stroll leisurely through a landscape. We tend to want to turn it into an opportunity for exercise or for catching up with friends. Take small steps and observe every plant and animal around you. Pay attention to the trees swaying above your head or the birds darting in and out of the bushes. What does the air smell like? What does the ground feel like beneath your feet? What do you hear? Even a small crackle of brush can indicate the presence of an animal nearby. Take breaks to stand still and take in your surroundings, or sit for five to ten minutes and see what emerges from your stillness.

4. Follow up. After the nature walk, discuss what you saw and heard with your fellow walkers. Consider keeping a nature journal where you record your observations for each walk, or you can share your findings in an app like ebird or iNaturalist.

Chapter 4

LAMENT AND THE CREATION

I looked on the earth, and lo, it was waste and void;
and to the heavens, and they had no light.
I looked on the mountains, and lo, they were quaking,
and all the hills moved to and fro.
I looked, and lo, there was no one at all,
and all the birds of the air had fled.
I looked, and lo, the fruitful land was a desert,
and all its cities were laid in ruins
before the LORD, *before his fierce anger.*
(Jeremiah 4:23–26)

When I was an idealistic eighteen-year-old, heading off to college and living away from my family for the first time, my only goal in life was to join the Peace Corps. I wanted to make a difference in the world, and the best way to do that was to help villagers somewhere in a remote jungle access clean water or farm sustainably. I wanted to major in environmental studies because I thought that was the best way to the Peace Corps and to saving the planet.

In my very first semester of college, I took Introduction to Environmental Studies, and the course almost broke my mind. In every single class, we were inundated with the gory details of the destruction humans have wrought on the planet and heard about how we were headed toward cataclysm if the world's governments did not make major changes to climate policy. Week after week was filled with this doom-and-gloom message: humans were the worst thing to happen to the earth and there was not much we as individuals could do about it. This was the fall of 2001, in the aftermath of the September 11 terror attacks, around the time when scientists finally had a clear picture of the full impact climate change was having on the planet but offered no plan for how to stop it. It was a bleak time to be studying the environment and for embracing adulthood in the uncertainty of the twenty-first century.

It took me a good ten more years of reading and learning to realize the situation might not be as dire as originally predicted and that small groups of committed people can and were doing things to alleviate climate change. At that time, I found myself paralyzed by guilt at my part in the environmental crisis, but I didn't have tools to move past it and toward something more positive. Instead, I coped with the situation by changing my major to biology, and I never took another environmental studies class. Instead of feeling so sad, I chose to focus on the amazing world of plants.

I ended up spending a good chunk of my college career collecting seeds and growing plants for ecological restoration projects, but it never occurred to me that by doing this I was taking action to mitigate climate change. I just enjoyed being around plants, watching them grow quietly in the greenhouse in the depths of winter, waiting for the spring, then gently placing them in the rich dark earth when it was warm enough. In that first semester ecology class, we had never talked about ecological restoration or what role we might play in it—we stayed stuck on what was going wrong.

What I realize now about the context of that course is that I didn't feel there was a place for my deep grief about the destruction of earth's ecosystems. If we had been given a chance to mourn together our collective loss, maybe I would have found more meaning and hope in the study of our fragile planet, and maybe I could have remained in the program. Instead, I left and found other outlets for my scientific mind. What stays with me most profoundly is that gut-wrenching sadness I felt and how helpless that reality made me feel. I know I'm not alone in feeling this way when confronted with the difficult realities of our fragile planet. Once we open ourselves up to the beauty and wonder of the natural world, our hearts are also broken open by all the devastation we find. Recentering the experiences of our bodies and emotions is crucial for coming to terms with the devastating effects of climate change on our world and for learning to live more gently on the planet.

Over the past twenty years, psychologists have focused on the central role of emotion in decision-making. In a 2015 review article for the *Annual Review of Psychology*, Jennifer S. Lerner and colleagues argued that there has been a revolution in the science of emotion in recent decades. They analyzed data from thirty-five years of research on emotion and decision-making, a topic that was largely ignored until the turn of the twenty-first century. Their analysis of hundreds of studies showed that the "research reveals that emotions constitute potent, pervasive, predictable, sometimes harmful and sometime beneficial drivers of decision making."[1] They noted that "many psychological scientists now assume that emotions are, for better or worse, the dominant driver of most meaningful decisions in life" as humans seek to avoid negative feelings and increase positive feelings, even when they are unaware of it.[2]

We tend to think of "emotional decisions" as a bad thing, something to be avoided, but it turns out that without emotions, people often make very poor decisions. In their analysis, Lerner and her team pointed to studies in which researchers found that individuals with damage to the area of the prefrontal cortex, which is involved in the processing of emotions, often made poor decisions because they could not accurately assess risk or make value judgments.[3]

We ignore the role of emotions in decision-making to our own peril, especially as it relates to motivating people to action related to climate change. All the facts and figures and grim statistics in the world don't necessarily change people's minds in the same way that surviving a hurricane or seeing a starving polar bear can. Naming these emotions is crucial as we seek to live well on this fragile planet, as we cannot help but feel things about the painful consequences we bear witness to, in our own communities and around the globe.

It's also important to recognize how we deal with this grief, anger, and other troublesome emotions—without losing hope—when we're confronted with the devastation wrought by climate change. It is easy to give in to despair when facing the plight of the earth and all its creatures, but working through grief can help us tap into deep reservoirs of hope, when we remember that God also mourns each loss.

Lament is a spiritual practice that provides an outlet for our deep grief through heartfelt words, usually in the form of a poem or song. Many of the psalms are laments, expressing distress or mourning the seeming absence of God in the face of disasters. Lament helps us give voice to our feelings of grief and anxiety and our experience of suffering. This can include the emotions that flow through us when we see a polluted river or a barren strip-mine site, or when we read about the disappearance of polar ice and the rise of sea levels. Lament helps us to live well on our fragile planet by giving us an outlet for these emotions and by keeping us from turning our backs in despair to the plight of the earth.

EMOTIONS FOR A SUFFERING PLANET

The crush of climate-change-induced anxiety creeping up around the world is real, and it is growing fast. A study by the American Psychological Association found that over two-thirds of adults in the United States have some degree of climate anxiety.[4] In some areas, climate change is posing an existential threat to survival, and there it's not as much an existential anxiety as it is a real human crisis unfolding. In North America, anxiety about climate change is often more of that existential variety, as we grieve over natural disasters happening throughout the world and wonder how our actions contribute to these events.

Speaking personally as a middle-class resident of the Midwest, I am buffered from the most severe effects of climate change. I live in a small, insulated house in a well-drained, forested neighborhood on a hill. I am at very low risk of flooding, forest fires, excess heat in the summer, and bitter cold in the winter. And yet, I am still sometimes overwhelmed by anxiety about what is happening elsewhere on the planet and my role in it. I know that many of the worst polluters and drivers of climate change are industry and government policy, and it sometimes seems there are few things ordinary citizens can do to influence the choices of these entities. But I drive my car on an almost daily basis—to the grocery store, to church, to visit family and friends—emitting greenhouse gases into the air. I also make choices about what food to buy, local or foreign, whether to fly places in an airplane, and how many

consumer goods I buy—the latest iPhone, that hiking backpack, yet another pair of shoes. Each of these decisions carries
an environmental impact, and that can begin to weigh on me
as I try to make (sometimes complicated) decisions that will
help everyone live well on this fragile planet.

In her recent book *Environmental Guilt and Shame*, environmental ethicist Sarah Fredericks sheds light on this phenomenon of climate anxiety, working to understand the role of
guilt and shame in either motivating or paralyzing action. She
notes that "emotions are often neglected or rejected compared
to rational arguments in environmental ethics such that ethical
knowledge informed by emotions is also discounted."[5] Like
Lerner and others, she advocates for the power of emotion in
decision-making regarding the environment, and she argues
that guilt and shame do motivate action but can also backfire
and lead to denial and hopelessness. Emotions are a natural
aspect of grieving for a planet in turmoil, and in the right context, they can cause people to change negative behaviors.

Central to her argument is the idea that there is no single
ideal solution to climate change. We are imperfect humans
living within imperfect cultural systems. This naturally leads
to guilt and shame when we fall short, but we have to come
to terms with the reality that we must always fail to some
degree in order to make any progress forward. Our problem,
at least in the modern West, is that we don't really know how
to deal with failure or imperfect outcomes. Indigenous theologian Randy Woodley argues similarly that white Americans
tend to jump to immediate action when they see a problem,
rather than to acknowledge the complexity of a situation and
recognize that a perfect solution is not always possible.[6] We
skip an important part of the process when we fail to listen to
and sit with our emotions.

Environmental philosopher Andreas Weber, like Fredericks, also urges us to acknowledge our limits and failures in trying to prevent ecological destruction. There is no utopia, no perfect solution: "We will find no way out of this misery for as long as we try to *solve* it . . . it must be endured and transformed."[7] This idea that there is a technology or solution to all of the world's problems misses the mark, and when failure looms, it is easy to fall into inaction and despair. Instead, Weber encourages people to recognize that "the world is a genuinely tragic place, and that the tragedy of it must be endured, because it cannot be shut down without simultaneously shutting down all of creation. Or rather: not endured but transformed into aliveness."[8] Life and death, light and darkness, are all bound up with one another. Death is a tragedy that leads to new life. We compound that tragedy when we try to cling to our own life and happiness at the expense of all others.

Some of the best spiritual resources for coming to terms with our emotional reactions to climate change are the creation stories. Creation stories are almost universal features of religious and cultural traditions, and for good reason. Humans have a deep need to understand where we came from, and how life came to be how it is. Creation stories bring to light what is most important about being human and about our relationship with God and the rest of the world.

CREATION

Our reading and interpretation of the two creation accounts in Genesis shape how we view the earth and our role in it, often dividing those who value creation as a sacred gift from God from those who believe God made the earth as a resource for humans to use as we wish. A faithful reading of these dense three chapters must go beyond the one verse

(Genesis 1:28), where God charges humanity to fill and sub-
due the earth.

In the first creation account (Genesis 1), there is a liturgical
retelling of the creation of the world as an act of worship—
God speaking things into being in peace and harmony. In the
second creation account (Genesis 2–3), we read a story of
humans living in a self-sustaining garden, where all food is
provided to them, but ultimately disobeying God by eating
from the forbidden tree. There are whole worlds contained in
these three chapters. They tell a story about where humanity
came from and how we came to be who we are. Both stories
make it clear that we come from the humus of the living earth
and from the breath of God, who breathes life into us and
speaks the whole world—a self-sustaining cosmos—into being.

When God began to create the heavens and the earth, "the
earth was a formless void and darkness covered the face of
the deep, while a wind from God swept over the face of the
waters" (Genesis 1:2). Theologian Catherine Keller has written a whole book on this second verse of Genesis, articulating
an entire theology based on these eleven Hebrew words. She
notes that while we so easily forget that chaos is at the heart
of creation, this chaotic substance of the deep, which is called
tehom in Hebrew, is the material God used to create.[9] This
view challenges the doctrine of *creatio ex nihilo*, or creation
from nothing.

She writes, "Christian theology, I argue, created this *ex
nihilo* at the cost of its own depth. It systematically and sym-
bolically sought to erase the chaos of creation."[10] She offers
an account of creation from "the *topos* of the Deep" rather
than from nothing, which opens up space for marginalized
groups and their theologies to be welcomed into the unfolding
of creation as an ongoing process.[11]

How we think about creation theology matters. For example, the doctrine of *creatio ex nihilo*, specifically, has been used to legitimize the whole colonial project of domination and subjugation of Indigenous peoples all over the world. As European explorers traveled to unknown-to-them continents, they viewed the Indigenous inhabitants they encountered as animals and their landscapes full of untapped resources, waiting to be "created" into a civilized society. In *Decolonizing Ecotheology*, theologians S. Lily Mendoza and George Zachariah write, "The European colonial theology of conquest is founded on the Genesis narratives of the primordial earth as 'void,' 'dark,' and 'deep,' and the Patristic creation theology of 'creation out of nothing,' legitimizing the vocation and mission of the chosen race to colonize the heathens and their lands."[12] Colonization was undoubtedly a theological act, a taking of the lands of others based on the capitalist desire for power and resources, but it was undergirded with a theology that legitimized this behavior within imperial Christianity.[13]

Keller offers a more biblically resonant alternative with her theology of *creatio ex profundis*, or creation from the depths. This concept draws heavily on Jewish and Kabbalistic theological traditions in addition to Christian theology, arguing ultimately that *creatio ex profundis* is more biblically accurate than the Christian doctrine of *creatio ex nihilo*. Rather than impose God's will on an empty nothingness, God creates from the dark depths of the waters, nurturing order and life out of a primordial soup.

This radically changes how we perceive the earth and our embodiment as part of it, because it means that the substance of the universe and God are in close relationship with one another, and that relationship persists. God is not a transcendent being creating from outside but forming from within.

Keller closes the book with the following words: "In beginning: a plurisingularity of universe, earth echoing chaos, dark
deep vibrating with spirit, creates."[14]

I still remember the mind-blowing moment in the first
ecotheology course I took in seminary, when our professor,
Dr. Carol Newsom, mapped out the first creation story on the
board as we read it out loud together. She made the following
diagram of degrees of separation:

Day 1: light from
darkness

Day 2: waters of sky from
waters of sea

Day 3: water from dry
land

Day 4: sun from moon, day
from night

Day 5: birds from fish

Day 6: earth creatures—
domestic and wild animals,
insects, humans

Each of the first three days of creation is an act of differentiation: the light from the darkness, the waters above from the
waters below, water from land. Then there is a second layer of
differentiation in the next three days: sun from moon, birds
from fish, and all types of earthbound creatures.

It's important to point out that, in this creation account, the
sky is understood to hold back the floodgates of a precarious
body of water above the earth. Perhaps because the sky was
blue, and rain fell from it at times, the early Israelites made
sense of their world through this imagery. In this context, the
differentiation of fish and birds, which at first glance might
seem an odd pairing, makes sense. The birds are the inhabitants of the sky, the dome beneath the waters, while the fish
are the inhabitants of the sea below. Also, birds would have
been seen in great flocks in wetlands of the ancient Middle
East, taking to the sky from the water, making their compari-
son to fish natural to the inhabitants of such landscapes.

The first creation story is an extended poetic liturgy, the perfect unfolding of a peaceful cosmos. It provided a stark contrast to the Babylonian creation story, which would have been well-known to the ancient Israelites. In the Babylonian account, the earth is created from an act of violence amid conflict, the ripping apart of the goddess Tiamat to make the substance of heaven and earth.[15] In the first Genesis creation account, however, God creates the earth by speaking words into the chaotic deep, bringing order and life. The earth is not created from the outcome of violence but is spoken and proclaimed wholly good. God also creates the earth to be self-sustaining, through plants that bear seed, so that it doesn't need constant divine intervention to function. God sets in motion the whole unfolding of the cosmos, proclaiming each portion good, or holy.

The second creation account found in Genesis 2:4–25 is less poetry and more folk story, recounting how God formed the first human "from the dust of the ground, and breathed into his nostrils the breath of life" (Genesis 2:7). In this telling, only the primordial water precedes the creation of the human. God plants a garden in Eden for the first human, full of rivers and green plants. Then God realizes that it isn't good for the human to be alone, and so creates all of the animals and brings them to the human to be named. In the end, God takes a rib from the human to make a woman, and Adam and Eve become human partners, tilling and keeping the garden together. As we know, this idyllic time was short-lived, with the serpent showing up as the trickster figure to suggest that God has lied to them about the tree of knowledge being deadly. Always curious as all humans are, Eve investigates by eating the fruit and giving it to Adam, which leads them to be cast out of the perfect garden to toil on the land and in childbirth.

So much theological baggage has been attached to the second creation story that it's easy for its original Hebrew context to be obscured and its meaning lost. When we peel back the layers, what remains is an agrarian story about how we came to be human, at once animal and separate from the rest of creation. Adam and Eve are originally tasked as the farmers of the garden of Eden, keeping it and tilling it. But the text implies that this was not an onerous task, and that the garden reflected a self-sufficient ecosystem where all organisms lived in balance with one another. It is only after Adam and Eve have been cast out that God curses Adam to a life of toil on the earth, farming only through hard work and the sweat of his brow.

The second creation story contains many etiologies, or explanations for why the world is the way it is: why snakes and humans have enmity for one another, why childbirth is painful, why humans are relegated to a life of toil in working the land. These outcomes aren't necessarily what God had in mind for the world, the story tells us, but they are the reality for the world as it is now.

Like all creation stories, these two accounts are attempts by the ancient peoples to make sense of their place in the cosmos. In the Hebrew tradition, humans have a special relationship with God. We are given a duty to protect the earth as well as to be receivers of special wisdom, whether that was God's original intention or not. There are certainly problematic elements to this framework, especially regarding gender roles and the language of dominion, but the creation stories do not speak alone; other parts of the Hebrew Bible make clear that the land is a gift from God and that sustenance from the land and the well-being of the earth itself is contingent on the behavior of the Hebrew people. If they succumb to a lust for wealth and become an unjust society, mistreating the poor and refugees, the land will be taken from them.

Dominion clearly comes only as part of an ethic of care and justice for all creation. God allows humans to dwell on the land and gain their sustenance from it, but only for as long as they are careful not to mistreat the other living beings that live on it, including the poor and marginalized in human society. The land is a gift that requires careful tending, not a resource to be used however they wish.

THE LAND BELONGS TO GOD: LAW AND THE UNDOING OF CREATION

After God delivers the Israelites from slavery in Egypt and leads them for a generation through the desert to a "land flowing with milk and honey" (Exodus 3:8), the Hebrew Bible makes clear the condition of justice and equity for their continued tenure in the land of Israel. The laws of Leviticus teach that God's gift of land is dependent on their ongoing actions—and the land remains above all a gift, not a possession. There is a clear connection between the social order and the ecological order; the Israelites owe their whole lives to God, and the only way to keep the land that supports their life is to uphold a just social system.[16]

We see this most clearly in two important concepts found in Leviticus: the sabbath of the land and the divine owner-ship of the land. In Leviticus 25:2–4, God calls the Israelites to observe a sabbath on the land every seventh year, during which they are instructed to let the land lie fallow. It is unclear whether this instruction was actually observed, as it would be untenable to not grow any food for an entire year, but the idea of letting land lie fallow had ecological value in that it allowed the fragile desert landscape to renew itself. Leviticus also makes it clear that God is the ultimate owner of the land and that the Israelites are only tenants of it—in Leviticus 25:23 God tells the people, "The land is mine; with me you are but aliens and tenants." There are other levitical laws concerning the buying and selling of the land, to ensure that it is equitably distributed and that no one falls into debt.

When the Israelites broke the covenant with God by abusing the land and not ensuring justice for all people, they believed that it was God who had caused them to be overtaken by foreign invaders and exiled from the land—rather than a consequence of their own failure. In the first part of the book of Jeremiah—a prophet who lived during the time when the Israelites were sent into exile—he warns the Israelites repeatedly of their unfaithfulness and the calamity that will result from it. In Jeremiah 4:23–26 the prophet in poetic language describes the potential unmaking of creation in a way that mirrors the creation story in Genesis 1. He writes:

> I looked on the earth, and lo, it was waste and void;
>> and to the heavens, and they had no light.
> I looked on the mountains, and lo, they were quaking,
>> and all the hills moved to and fro.
> I looked, and lo, there was no one at all,
>> and all the birds of the air had fled.
> I looked, and lo, the fruitful land was a desert,
>> and all its cities were laid in ruins
>> before the LORD, before his fierce anger.

In these words of the prophet, each act of creation in Genesis 1 is revoked until there is nothing left. Theologian Ellen Davis compares Jeremiah's vision of the fruitful land becoming barren and creation being unmade to witnessing a mountaintop removal site in eastern Kentucky. She writes, "Mountaintop removal is an emblematic act. Along with nuclear testing, this is the most dramatic rupture of the created order that North Americans have effected on our own continent. In Appalachia, the oldest part of our continent—the place where God began work on our quadrant of the globe—we are proceeding to return God's handiwork to utter formlessness and waste, *tohu wabohu*, stripping bare one of the most biologically diverse temperate forest regions in the world."[17]

It is important to note that in addition to its ecological devastation, this unmaking of the earth is equally devastating for the human communities that live near mountaintop removal sites because it poisons their drinking water and, in some cases, creates landslides that cover houses and farms in toxic sludge.[18] Jeremiah's warning is perhaps as much for us as it was for the Israelites of his day.

Poet and pastor Tamara Shantz reimagines the Jubilee year in Leviticus 25 in her own Canadian context as a settler resident of the land that once belonged to the Haudenosaunee people. She writes, "I am disappointed in the Jubilee. / I turn to Leviticus 25 / expecting a damning critique / of the colonial enterprise." But instead, she finds that the Jubilee is only for the Israelites, and the Indigenous inhabitants are noticeably absent.[19] In pondering the text as she cycles around her city, Shantz realizes that she is not the Israelite. It is the Haudenosaunee who are "carrying the heartbeat of Jubilee" with their wisdom that the land is a being to whom we all belong.[20]

In this creative reimagining, it is the original inhabitants of her land who hold the wisdom of the land as a gift. In the end of the poem, she asks to be liberated from a mindset that calculates silently the value of her own land, this colonial framework that sees only property where others recognize all things as gifts.

Shantz also raises the important issue of the original inhabitants of the land of Israel, the Canaanites. The book of Joshua chronicles the victory of the Israelites over the Canaanites as they come to possess the land, including depictions of horrific violence and genocide against the original inhabitants. Many Indigenous and African diaspora theologians rightly argue that the Exodus story is complicated by the genocide and stealing of land that follows, and that it is a poor basis for liberation theology because of the inherent bias of the writers of the Bible against Indigenous inhabitants.

Archaeological evidence indicates that the first Hebrew people emerged from the Canaanites and that the Exodus story was written much later during the exilic period as a generative myth to explain the beginning of Israelite religion. The fact remains, though, that in the book of Joshua, genocide of the local people is portrayed as the will of God. The Bible can be complicated and disquieting, and not all of it seems to us like the word of God.

It is helpful to remember that the writers of the Bible were fallible, imperfect humans who recorded stories that reinforced their beliefs and customs. The mandates of Jubilee, sabbath for the land, and debt cancellation included in Leviticus are meaningful to how I understand my faith tradition even though the violence of Joshua is not. The Old Testament contains some unsettling imagery amidst the stories of God's loving presence on the earth, but for me the troubling violence of the Old Testament is tempered by Jesus' profound witness to the power and goodness of nonviolence in his actions throughout his ministry. The New Testament offers a vision of what the restoration of shalom might look like, both in the life of Jesus and in the stories of his early followers.

RE-CREATION: THE COSMIC RESTORATION OF PAUL

It's often assumed that the primary theme of Paul's letters is salvation and the building of the community of Christ. But Paul also had quite a bit to say about restoration on a more cosmic scale. Looking at the letters of Paul through an ecological lens, we can see that creation plays a central role in Paul's vision of liberation and renewal.[21] Two passages where this more universal vision of restoration is most visible are Romans 8:18–23 and Colossians 1:15–20. These passages and others make clear that Paul envisioned redemption through Christ on a cosmic scale. Christ came not only to show humans how to live but to restore a creation that had become subject to decay and futility.

Romans 8:18–23 offers a beautiful meditation on living hopefully in a suffering world. The redemption depicted in these verses is not only for humans but for all living things. Creation is named five times and plays an audible role, "groaning" for redemption in verse 22. Paul's understanding was that creation became subject to decay after Adam and Eve were expelled from the garden. Their sin was cosmic in scale, and so the redemption would also be cosmic. Whether or not you hold to the doctrine of original sin as Augustine imagined it, the idea that the earth suffers when humans sin makes perfect sense if we understand sin as that which separates us from God and the biotic community, humans included.

Sin, in the larger sense of human lust for power and wealth, does indeed subject the whole creation to futility. In our constant craving for more, we plunder the resources of the earth without regard for its sacredness. When Paul writes that all creation groans, the verb prefixes in the Greek mean literally that creation was groaning *together* and laboring *together*, all living things groaning in labor pains in the process of birthing the children of God (v. 19).[22] To borrow the words of biblical scholar Vicky Balabanski, creation is "an active and generous subject leaning together with humans toward a shared future of freedom and glory."[23] It is also important to note that Paul's vision of renewal is not a redemption *from* the body but *of* the body.[24] Our bodies are important, not as chains weighing us down, but part of God's holy creation.

Colossians 1:15–20 is often called a Christ hymn, and it is thought to be a piece of liturgy used by the early church and quoted by Paul in his letter. The verses have a symmetry to them, beginning with depicting the creation of the world in the first two verses and moving to redemption in the second half, with key words repeated in both halves. Here Paul makes the point that Christ is the unifying force of the cosmos, the "firstborn of all creation" (v. 15) and in whom "all things hold together" (v. 17). Jesus is the source of life for the whole creation, not just humans, and this makes the implications of his resurrection cosmic in scale. In verses 19 and 20, Paul wrote, "For in him all the fullness of God was pleased to dwell, and through him God was pleased to reconcile to himself all things, whether on earth or in heaven. . . ." These words intensify the cosmic nature of redemption even more, reminding us that God dwells in all of life: oceans, cardinals, and maple trees along with humans.

Paul's vision of this cosmic restoration, so resonant in these two passages, is found in other letters as well. It is clear that he not only preached a gospel of humans living in community with one another; he also believed that Jesus came to redeem and restore humanity's relationship with all of creation as well. Though it would be anachronistic to read our current global climate crisis into the words of Paul, his letters are a living testament of our faith, and we find new meaning and wisdom in the Bible for our own current situation.

FEELING THE PULSE OF A SENTIENT EARTH

When I take time to deeply absorb these creation and re-creation stories, I am immediately brought back to my own embodied experience. I notice the birds singing from the trees around me as I sit outside reading on the porch. When I am inside, I take time to feel the grain of the wood floor on my bare feet as I walk through the house. When washing dishes, I feel the cool water from the tap flowing over my soapy hands and I wonder about the journey the water took to get from the river up the road into my pipes. In short, I feel more alive and present, which leads into a deep gratitude for the bounty of my life.

I am also reminded that feelings of guilt and sadness are a natural part of grieving for an earth in crisis. I hug my eighteen-year-old self, who found it all too much, and then I keep moving forward. I plant ferns and Solomon's seal in my yard. I guard the maple sapling sprouting up from the flower bed instead of cutting it down for being in the wrong spot. I walk to the grocery store for a few items instead of driving, and I spend the whole time noticing the people and landscape around me.

There is no perfect solution to climate change that will save the earth and let us keep all our precious technological advancements. There is no way to resurrect all the species that are dying off each day. Lofty promises of politicians aren't of any comfort to someone who lost their whole family to flooding from a hurricane. Every action we take is imperfect, because the world is imperfect. But we keep moving forward anyway.

PUTTING IT INTO PRACTICE: LAMENT FOR THE EARTH

Part of coming to terms with imperfection and complexity is reexamining our collective identity and values and envisioning a new way forward. Rituals are a primary tool for addressing the damage we have caused—helping people grieve for what we have already lost as a planet and imagining a more hopeful future. Rituals must make space for those uncomfortable emotions. We need not fear those emotions, because they are important aspects of our inner life and existence. Ritual offers a way to collectively confess our sins and change our ways as a community of imperfect humans. Coming to grips with guilt and shame through ritual and other communal activities is crucial in motivating change and in being more fully who we are as beautiful, imperfect organisms.

Lament is one such ritual that helps us deal with our pain and sense of loss by putting our emotions into words. The laments in the Bible, both in the Psalms and Lamentations, are poetic offerings by the Israelites to God. In lament they express grief, outrage, despair, and hope, in the context of community. Laments are a kind of prayer that helps us channel our emotions in a way that transforms us and our community.

It is part of our modern worldview to want to leap to action when we see injustice or tragedy happening in the world, but it is important to first spend time listening and lamenting. Randy Woodley has written about this phenomenon, and he urges European-descended people not to ask, "What can we do?" before spending time listening and lamenting the current reality. He writes, "European minds first want to know and then they immediately want to fix it, quickly. They believe they can fix everything; this is part of the worldview."[25] Instead, we ought first to spend a long time listening to what the problems are and becoming aware of our role in them. Then, we ought to come together in community to lament and memorialize.

When our lament is genuine, it can lead to a deep compassion for other beings. When we lament, we feel on a visceral level the suffering of humans, animals, and even plants. This is the root of compassion that makes other actions possible.

In the Bible, laments were protests to God about a particular tragedy that was unfolding. They were prayers requesting an answer, from wounded communities seeking solace by looking to God for help. When writing your lament, you can model it on one of the psalms or create something entirely new.

Psalm 3 is a good example of a lament. It begins with a cry to God about the many foes that surround the psalmist. Then in verse 3, the theme shifts to trusting in God. The psalmist says, "But you, O LORD, are a shield around me." In subsequent verses the psalmist testifies that God is a sustainer and deliverer. The psalm ends with a request for redemption from the enemy and for a blessing. Other psalms that include lament are Psalms 13, 17, 25, 74, and 89.

Your lament can be for a specific element or animal, or for something more general like the earth as a whole or the oceans. It can be in the form of a poem, but it doesn't have to. A painting can even be a kind of lament, through images instead of words. Feel free to get creative and share what you make with your family or church community. You could even consider having a service of lamentation in which multiple people share what they have created.

Chapter 5

RECONNECTING WITH THE EARTH AND OUR BODIES

Sacred Words

You set the earth on its foundations,
so that it shall never be shaken.
You cover it with the deep as with a garment;
the waters stood above the mountains. (Psalm 104:5–6)

I praise you, for I am fearfully and wonderfully made.
Wonderful are your works;
that I know very well.
My frame was not hidden from you,
when I was being made in secret,
intricately woven in the depths of the earth.
(Psalm 139:14–15)

In April 2020, shortly after the first lockdown of the pandemic began in North America, several members of my congregation started a poetry discussion group via Zoom. This video-conferencing platform helped us connect with one another since we no longer saw each other on Sunday mornings, and it was also a way to deal collectively with our anxiety and grief during a tumultuous time. Each week, one member of the group would read a poem and tell the others what was meaningful to them about it. The experience was cathartic and thought-provoking; in the subsequent year, I learned more about my fellow congregants than I had in six previous years of attending church with them. What was most powerful about this simple act of fellowship was that we had a chance to give voice to our many emotions as we mulled over each poem.

Poetry is, at its heart, an emotional act, a gift from one person to another. When we try to dissect poetry using logical arguments or set frameworks, it quickly loses its vibrancy. This is why many of us struggled with poetry in English class. We weren't taught how to write poetry, how to pour out our souls onto the page in a few words. Instead, we were taught concepts like imagery and symbolism, and then we proceeded to sap the life out of every worthwhile poem set in front of us.

What was important on those quiet Tuesday nights during the pandemic, with each of us in our tiny square on a computer screen, were the emotional connections we made with a work of art and with one another. We used the poets' words to help dredge up our own words so we could begin to tell stories about our collective life during this difficult time.

The poetry found in the Psalms contains these same heartfelt emotional expressions, evidence of both the grief and joy that the ancient Israelites felt as they navigated their lives together. In this chapter we will use the poetry of the Psalms as a way into greater connection with the earth and with our own bodies. Psalm 139 specifically is helpful for making sense of our own embodiment in the context of the brokenness of the world and the mysterious presence of the Sacred in our lives.

An important part of reorienting our lives to the cycles of the earth is to become aware of the miracle of our embodiment. Humans are literally made up of the stuff of earth. The food we eat, the coffee we drink, and the air we breathe are a reminder of our earthly rootedness. These are also reminders that we are connected to many other humans throughout the world—the farmers who harvest the produce we consume, the migrant worker who picks the berries we put in our yogurt, the cow that provides us with milk, and the grower who harvests our coffee beans or tea leaves half a world away. An important part of living well on this fragile planet is understanding that we are woven intricately into global webs, and rejoicing in our embodiment reminds us of this connection.

POETRY AND THE BIBLE: WORDS THAT EVOKE THE PRESENCE OF GOD

Before we delve into the evocative language of the Psalms, it's helpful to have a bit of background on how poetry can help us frame our faith and beliefs in a free and more vibrant way. Theopoetics offers one lens for this important work. It is often defined as a way of doing theology that relies on emotional and spiritual connection with a text rather than mere logic. When we can connect with a scripture text or a spiritual experience on an emotional or embodied level, we invite the Sacred into our lives in a more intimate way. We interact with sacred words and with God, wrestling with the ideas we find in the Bible in an attempt to create a closer connection to God. We are always limited by our language when we attempt to speak about the Divine, and we ought to recognize these limits instead of presuming to have the mystery all figured out.

Theopoetics scholar L. Callid Keefe-Perry writes that "we were all—even theologians and pastors—made to dance, not merely to think about dancing."[1] If engaging in theology is like thinking about dancing, we ought to actually participate in the experience, which is what theopoetics is all about.

The values espoused by theopoetics are helpful for this project of a re-embodied faith grounded in the earth. Theopoetics first involves an embodied emotional experience of God, not simply an intellectual exercise in speaking about God. The way we give words to our beliefs is more accessible through art than through logic, because, at its core, faith is an emotional response to our experience in a world of love and loss, trauma and joy. Poetry reflects deep emotional conviction, expressed through evocative imagery and metaphor. Using theopoetics as a way to engage with God helps us encounter the sacred in the same way, by engaging this emotional connection.

Brazilian scholar Rubem Alves was one of the first theologians to adopt theopoetics as a new way of expressing theological convictions. He fled Brazil during the 1964 coup, after he was named an enemy of the state, to study for his doctoral degree at Princeton. As a refugee from a developing country, Alves did not feel that he fit into the academic theology culture of Princeton and chafed against the scholarly entrapment of God. Theopoetics offered something more freeing—as he describes it: "God is the Wind: it comes, it goes, it cannot be put in paper cages or word cages. . . . After it goes the only thing which is left is the memory of its touch on my skin. I can only speak about this: reverberations on my body, as it is touched by the Wind."[2] True encounters with the Holy don't fit neatly into theological categories, he found. They excite and terrify; they change how we think about ourselves and God. Theopoetics gives voice to that more direct experience.

Theopoetics also gives voice to the beliefs of ordinary Christians rather than professional theologians, giving everyone language with which to speak of their encounter with the sacred. Anabaptist theologian Scott Holland notes that even though the term theopoetics isn't normally used by ordinary people, "all experientially inspired articulation of God—via popular music, over kitchen tables, in novels, movies, etc.—is a form of theopoetic expression."[3] These expressions of belief, even though they aren't written or spoken in an academic style, still represent authentic theological discourse. Our words about God are always piecemeal and inadequate to express the grandeur and majesty of the Sacred. When I stand next to a raging waterfall or lie down under a dome of stars, the words that most often come to my lips are ones of thanksgiving and awe to find myself in the midst of such beauty. The psalms come from this same place of a firsthand experience of faith—both gratitude for the bounty of creation and anguish for times of famine and war.

REINHABITING OUR BODIES: FORMED BY GOD

The book of Psalms is a collection of poems and songs composed over hundreds of years to meet the needs of the ancient Israelites worshiping in Jerusalem.[4] Because they were used in the context of worship, usually as sung or chanted liturgy, the psalms capture the deeply human side of faith in their expressions of joy, gratitude, and woundedness. And because they were used by a specific people in a specific time and place, they also reflect a very different worldview from our own. They are examples of theopoetic reflection, a lived theology that captures the messiness and beauty of life rather than abstract expositions about God. We find a clear example of this in Psalm 139. Its 24 verses depict a God who is intimately present in human lives and knowledgeable about our embodied existence.

The psalm begins, "O LORD, you have searched me and known me. You know when I sit down and then I rise up; you discern my thoughts from far away" (v. 1–2). In just these first few lines we are confronted with a God who is not in some distant, ethereal heaven, but close by, knowing both our thoughts and the movements of our bodies. God surrounds us and protects us, as verse 5 captures eloquently: "You hem me in, behind and before, and lay your hand upon me."

When I read these verses, they evoke an emotional response of comfort, reminding me that I am always surrounded by the presence of God. This use of tangible imagery is part of the power of theopoetic reflection. It helps create a clear image in our minds of what God's presence feels like. Even when I feel the deep anguish of grief or the sting of exclusion, I am not alone. At the same time, God also shares in my moments of profound happiness and contentment.

Verses 7–12 illustrate that we can go nowhere beyond the scope of God. "Where can I go from your spirit? Or where can I flee from your presence?" the psalmist asks in verse 7. "If I take the wings of the morning and settle at the farthest limits of the sea, even there your hand shall lead me, and your right hand shall hold me fast" (v. 9–10). We see here that God is with us in all times and places.

I am particularly drawn to the image of God's hand holding me—this is a tangible illustration, calling up memories of being held by a parent when I was a child. These kinds of emotions help me connect with the love of God much more than reading a statement of faith or a catechism.

In the second half of the psalm, the imagery shifts to our own creation. In verse 13 the psalmist writes, "For it was you who formed my inward parts; you knit me together in my mother's womb." This is followed in verse 14 by, "I praise you, for I am fearfully and wonderfully made." Because God is the force who shaped us, the Sacred is present in all of creation, always surrounding us and suffusing us, just as God suffuses the whole cosmos.

In verse 15, to reiterate the role of God in our creation, the psalmist writes, "My frame was not hidden from you, when I was being made in secret, intricately woven in the depths of the earth." This harkens back to the second creation story, when God forms Adam from the soil and breathes life into him. This is a powerful reminder that we are created from the stuff of the earth as well as in our mother's womb. Our bodies are formed from and sustained by the plants, animals, and air of the earth. This tangible metaphor helps us remember our connection to this fragile planet that we inhabit.

In the imagery of these verses is an emphasis on the body being formed by God and a reminder that God is present with us everywhere in the physical universe. It's not our thoughts or prayers or rituals that bind us together with God but our very being.

Verses 17 and 18 bring in the idea of God's thoughts: "How weighty to me are your thoughts, O God! How vast the sum of them! I try to count them—they are more than the sand." God's thoughts and our bodies are thoroughly intertwined in a kind of cosmic blend. We are to contemplate what God contemplates and remember our smallness, even as God remembers our infinite worth and the intricate care with which it took to form us. Verse 18 concludes with, "I come to the end—I am still with you." Not even death can separate us from God.

When we read the psalms closely and recognize how their beautiful poetry is its own valid theological expression, the words have the power to deepen our faith, as we enter the stream of these ancient verses. The psalms portray a universe that is full of both majesty and pain, a creation suffused with God's holy presence in every life. These words are a reminder that to live faithfully is to acknowledge the intricate beauty of creation and to work to protect and restore it. The psalms don't speak in abstract concepts about the nature of God; through poetry they remind us of our humanity and the powerful presence of God in our midst.

WHAT KEEPS US FROM WHOLENESS

What keeps us from realizing this beautiful psalm's vision of shalom, of wholeness, in the microcosm of our bodies, in our own lives? There are several ways we could answer that question, but the biggest impediment to feeling our deep connectedness to God and the earth is mind-matter dualism.

Dualism is a fundamental part of the Western philosophical inheritance and one of the most pervasive mindsets we have received from this culture. Dualism expresses an ancient bias, going all the way back to Plato's conception of the person being steered by two horses—one of the mind and one of the body.

But for the most prominent proponent of dualistic thinking, we turn to sixteenth-century French philosopher René Descartes. As discussed in chapter 3, Descartes is the author of the famous maxim, "I think, therefore I am." With this simple phrase and the mindset that came with it, he separated the world into two halves: those who think, and that which does not. Dualistic thinking keeps us from feeling at home in our own bodies and from bonding with nonhuman beings, because we see both as less important than our mental life. When we value ourselves primarily for our ability to think, we miss out on the more visceral connections with the earth and with our own experience of embodiment.

Though many have since offered better philosophies, dualism has continued to define our thinking—while periodically receiving new elements as new information or technologies emerge. For example, the relatively recent surge in research on the brain's role in the experience of consciousness has established a new form of dualism—the separation between the brain and the body. Current scientific understanding suggests that our brains are in ultimate control of our bodies, which are essentially just water and cells taking cues from the brain, the ultimate center of power and knowledge. This simplistic notion fails to take into account the intelligence that resides in the body. It also fails to recognize the reality that our brains are deeply intertwined with the rest of our body through a vast nervous system that is able to wire itself together in ways we are only beginning to understand.

Our bodies are sacred. They are places of both pain and pleasure, and our sensations help us connect to God just as much as our minds do. The sharp bite of a grapefruit on my tongue, or the gentle softness of moss underneath my fingers are reminders of the joy that my body feels when interacting with the created world around me. When I hold the hand of a small child or give a hug to a friend, I am reminded that God loves me in these same tangible ways.

Dualism also reinforces the hierarchy that places humans at the pinnacle of creation, with animals and plants far below us. This is not the mindset of the Bible, though. As we explored in previous chapters, creation in the Bible is fully alive. Hills sing and trees rejoice. Animals are messengers of truth. As it is for many Indigenous communities, for the ancient Israelites the world was vibrantly animate and alive, regardless of what created thing might have a brain or not.

In the Bible, thinking and speaking are not solely the ability of humans. In the same way, we cannot be truly embodied creatures on this sentient earth without coming to terms with this dualism that is our cultural inheritance. Thinking dualistically is a hard habit to break and involves a creative reimagining of our place in the world and of our own embodiment.

In order to break out of this mindset and reinhabit our bodies and landscapes, we must develop a renewed understanding of the concepts of thought and mind. We are not beings in isolation in a mechanical universe—we shape and are shaped by our surroundings. We respond to the constant changes in our surroundings with our whole body, sensing changes in terrain as we walk or in temperature as we work. Our skin is energized by hundreds of thousands of nerve fibers that sense every aspect of the landscape around us and adapt accordingly.

It is also important to remember that even the development of the human brain is intrinsically linked to the context of the environment. Humans are whole beings, enmeshed in a web of relationships within the ecosystem. Environmental philosopher David Abrams writes, "It is difficult, if not impossible, to conceive of how a mindful brain could have arisen except as an attribute of a muscled and sensing organism—how a brain could evolve independent of a breathing body fending for itself in the biosphere."[5]

In other words, our brains were formed in intimate connection with our bodies, which are in constant communication with the land around us. Our brains are an outgrowth of cold wind and birdsong, steep mountain slopes and gentle sunrises. Our true home is not in some ethereal mental realm, but knee-deep in the beautiful muck of the earth. When we feel at home in our bodies and on the earth, we are more aware of our connection to the sacred creation and to the Creator.

PUTTING IT INTO PRACTICE: WRITING YOUR OWN PSALM

If we want to live differently—to live well—on this fragile planet, we must do the work of changing our mindsets and rejecting those aspects of culture that keep us from connecting with God and one another. One way of disentangling ourselves from these mindsets is to share stories of our embodiment and enmeshment in the wider world, through poetry. Poetry helps us express our feelings about God in a different way than the rational argument of theology or the recounting of historical tradition. And poetry doesn't have to be eloquent or wordy to hold the light of truth. It is simply an act of recording our wonder, our pain, our joy, or our sorrows using memories and metaphors. Our creative act mirrors God's own continuing creativity in the unfolding of the universe.

The Jewish tradition of midrash is one such creative process. Midrash is a sort of interpretation of the biblical text that is meant to draw out a theological point or make a text accessible to an audience. Midrash is a way of being in relationship with a particular biblical text. Writing your own psalm is a kind of midrash on the original book of Psalms, a way of relating with the poetry of an ancient people.

As I write this, it is midsummer in Ohio and the fireflies are putting on a silent fireworks show nightly, their tiny glowing green bodies zipping through the darkness at the edge of the forest, blinking out a welcome to the warmth of the world. Every evening before bed, I go out and stand in the middle of the yard in awe as their blinking winged forms encircle me. The longer I watch, the more I see, as my eyes become accustomed to their faint light. In the light trails they leave behind I experience the words that God speaks through the landscape, words of joy and abundance.

They remind me that I already have all that I need. I experience the feeling of enoughness, of contentment. Tomorrow, more work awaits, and I will have worldly cares to attend to, but tonight the whole earth feels alive, and I am immersed in it. Though some nights I simply try to listen to what the night might be trying to tell me, some nights I am moved to attempt to put my experience into words, a poetic reflection on abundance.

There are psalms about many different emotional experiences, from gratitude to lament. The imagery of the psalms—sheep, mountains, singing with musical instruments—were taken from the daily life of the ancient Israelites.

For your own psalm, first think about what emotional experience you want to capture. What are some ordinary elements from your everyday life that evoke feelings of joy or gratitude? Or, are you in the midst of a difficult life change, or coping with a recent loss? What do these things feel like in your body? How is God present or absent from your midst? What do you most wish you could say to God? Do you have a message for your family or church community? Write it down, with as little self-consciousness as you can muster. This can be between you and God—you don't need to impress anyone with your beautiful words. If you'd like to share it with others, that's great too.

Hearing how God speaks and moves in the lives of others can be a powerful way of experiencing God in our own lives and can help us to imagine and embody new ways to live well on this fragile planet.

Chapter 6

RECONNECTING
WITH THE HOLY

Practicing Sabbath

Remember the sabbath day, and keep it holy. Six days you shall labor and do all your work. But the seventh day is a sabbath to the LORD your God; you shall not do any work—you, your son or your daughter, your male or female slave, your livestock, or the alien resident in your towns. For in six days the LORD made heaven and earth, the sea, and all that is in them, but rested the seventh day; therefore the LORD blessed the sabbath day and consecrated it. (Exodus 20:8–11)

As we seek to read the Bible faithfully and live well on our fragile planet by reconnecting to the biblical authors' pervasive sense of the aliveness of the earth, we can look to the art of sabbath rest as a tangible practice that helps ground us more firmly in the natural world.

The practice of honoring the Sabbath by refraining from work goes all the way back to Moses and the earliest days of the Hebrew people as they wandered in the desert. Jews and Christians are called to rest from work on the seventh day because that is what God did on the seventh day of creation. It is a reminder that we were not made for work; we were made for joy. Observance of the Sabbath was also a reminder to the Israelites that they had been slaves without rest in the land of Egypt and that God had delivered them from that life. The great Jewish theologian Rabbi Abraham Joshua Heschel calls the Sabbath "a palace in time," arguing that it is the pinnacle of the week, a time to be present with God and family, a taste of eternity.[1] Sabbath offers a time to rest from our constant pursuit of more.

When we are able to experience our lives as embodied and enmeshed in the whole web of creation, that experience has repercussions for how we act in the world. The ancient practice of Sabbath keeping is a way to rest from consumerism, to learn how to be with God, how to be still and appreciate the created world. Sabbath offers us a way into joy and wonder, as we slow down and pay attention to the present moment, recognizing the abundance of God and cultivating a sense of enoughness.

All of this helps us step outside of the dominant consumer culture, if only temporarily. The church community can then serve as a countercultural place of refuge. By Sabbath keeping I do not mean it in its past connotation as refraining from playing cards, drinking, or doing business. I mean it in a much deeper way, as a time to slow down and reconsider our lives from a different perspective. Heschel reminds us that humans are created for the Sabbath, for communion with God. It is our true home, outside of work and capitalist striving.

Practicing Sabbath also reminds us that life is a gift from God, and that we are part of the gift economy of the natural world. All the elements we need for survival—sunlight, food, water—are given freely by the earth. As we receive nourishment from the earth, so we also give nourishment to the rest of the biome. Hoarding the gifts of creation is a violation against nature and against God.

The Bible is full of passages reminding and encouraging us to embrace a sense of enoughness, or more with less, as a guiding principle in life. In the Exodus story, the Israelites were provided for in the wilderness, with daily manna. It is for this reason that Leviticus later mandates a Sabbath not just for all people but also for the land God had delivered them to. This served as a reminder that the earth and all that is in it belongs ultimately to God.

Norman Wirzba in *This Sacred Life* explains that creation stories "communicate the character or essence of reality,"[2] and the fact that the first creation story in Genesis ends with a day when God rests is crucial in understanding the kind of world that God wants us to inhabit. After creating the world, God wanted to rest in it, to experience its delight. Wirzba argues, "When God hallows this day of divine rest, what God is doing is saying that the climax and goal of life are achieved when people come into the presence of places and creatures and find there the love and joy of God at work."[3]

People were not made to be cogs in the machine of global capitalism. We were created for both meaningful work and generative rest, to enjoy being part of the vibrant green planet as we care for it and for one another. This is an important part of what it looks like to live well on this fragile planet.

THE ANXIETY OF CHRONOLOGICAL TIME

We have looked already at how modern Western culture is obsessed with time and its closely related notion of progress. This sense of chronological time, we saw, is an abstraction that separates humans from the present moment and keeps them from experiencing the presence of God. But knowing that doesn't always keep us from feeling the anxiety of chronological time in our daily lives.

As a child of parents who were usually running late, I was obsessed with being on time to everything. I worried about getting to school on time, getting to church on time, meeting friends on time, much to the bewilderment of the rest of my family. Part of it was an anxiety about getting into trouble if I was late, but another part was not wanting to let people down and wanting to be seen as a responsible person. Because no one else in my family seemed particularly bothered by these things, I felt like I needed to manage all of them in order for us as a group to get anywhere, much to their consternation.

It never occurred to me, until well into adulthood, that the world would keep spinning if I was a few minutes late, and that people usually have a certain amount of grace about lateness. Still to this day, if I'm stuck in traffic or delayed in leaving to get somewhere, my heart starts racing and my teeth start grinding at all the slow drivers on the road, wishing they would just get out of my way.

It's incredibly difficult to pull myself from the grip of beholdenness to punctuality demanded by chronological time. My anxiety at being late separates me from being truly aware of the present moment and the people around me. I see the drivers of slower cars only as impediments to my progress, rather than as other people who are also on a journey and living out their own stories.

A friend recently reminded me that during his ministry Jesus walked everywhere he went, at a slow pace that allowed him to talk with fellow travelers, notice the landscape around him, and make friends with the animals he encountered. In our car-addicted society, walking is typically relegated to those who have the fewest resources—a last resort for getting from one place to another, often on cracked sidewalks next to busy roadways. It's easy to forget that the pace of walking is the pace of life for many humans on this planet, and that Jesus probably had some of his best insights about life while walking from village to village.

Fortunately, there is a way out of this anxiety of chronological time, and Christian tradition offers tangible rituals and scriptures that help us step out of "the illusion of chronological time and pay deep attention to the bubbling up of the present and the cyclical times of the rest of the natural world."[4]

Prayer, in all its forms, is one way of reconnecting with the wideness of the present moment; it grounds us in the love of God and love of one another when we share our joys and our sorrows, or when we simply sit and listen for the voice of God to speak to us. Similarly, the rituals of worship also help us step out of the anxiety of chronological time and into sacred moments with the gathered community, when we hear Scripture read, celebrate communion, or mark life transitions through marriage and baptism.

This chapter focuses specifically on the notion of sabbath as a way to lessen the grip of chronological time and the energy demanded by Western notions of progress and productivity. Sabbath is a foundational Christian practice and a reminder that we were created for joy and love, not for labor alone. In the first creation story in Genesis, God rests on the seventh day after creating the world, in order to savor its beautiful perfection. God instructs the Israelites to keep the Sabbath as a reminder that rest is a key aspect of life, and a reminder that they were delivered from a life of endless toil in Egypt.

In Greek there are two words that connote a sense of time, but each has a slightly different meaning. *Kairos,* which means "the right point of time, the proper time or season of action, the exact or critical time,"[5] refers to an opportune time, or in the New Testament, the time when God acts or intervenes (see Mark 1:15).

Cronos, on the other hand, refers to "a definite time, a while, a period, a season . . . periods of time with chronological accuracy."[6] When people in Western culture talk about time, it is mostly this second type that we mean. *Cronos* has a quantitative quality to it, marking off specific amounts of time, or a certain point in time, whereas *kairos* is more qualitative, describing a moment filled with possibility, a point outside of chronological time. Sabbath, in Jewish tradition, is a particular segment of chronological time, but it has a *kairos* feel to it—Sabbath is meant to help usher us into an experience of time that is slower and more sacred than ordinary time, providing a space in the span of a day in which to pause and reflect.

THE JOY OF SABBATH

If you grew up during the era of a state-mandated weekly day of rest, with stores and even parks closed every Sunday—or if your family observed it this way—the word *Sabbath* might bring to mind a strict interpretation of a day in which no fun was to be had. When I use the term *sabbath*, I am not advocating for a return to this type of practice. Sabbath can happen at any time, and for any span of time.

According to Jewish tradition, the Sabbath stretches from sunset on Friday until the first stars appear in the sky on Saturday evening. It is a span of time determined by the changing seasons, with a longer sabbath on Friday evening in the winter, and a longer sabbath on Saturday during those lingering long days of summer. For most Christians, sabbath refers to the daylight hours of Sunday, or even more specifically, just Sunday morning, when we're at church. For the many who work in healthcare, retail, food service, and transportation, sabbath is whatever day you happen to be off work, if at all.

Honoring the Sabbath is among the first five commandments God gave Moses on Mt. Sinai. In Exodus 20:8–11 we read:

> Remember the sabbath day, and keep it holy. Six days you shall labor and do all your work. But the seventh day is a sabbath to the LORD your God; you shall not do any work—you, your son or your daughter, your male or female slave, your livestock, or the alien resident in your towns. For in six days the LORD made heaven and earth, the sea, and all that is in them, but rested the seventh day; therefore the LORD blessed the sabbath day and consecrated it.

This paragraph-long explanation shows us how sabbath rest is built into the design of creation. We were made for rest, not for constant toil. When we build our industrial society around maximizing profit—when we accept this as the purpose of our being—both humans and the earth suffer.

Perhaps the most well-known prophetic voice of the power of sabbath is Abraham Joshua Heschel (quoted earlier in the chapter), a Hasidic rabbi and professor of ethics and Jewish mysticism. He also worked closely with Martin Luther King during the civil rights movement in the 1960s. He wrote a short but powerful book called simply *The Sabbath* to counteract what he felt was an apathy about sabbath observance among his fellow Jews during the post-war period of economic expansion in the United States. He hoped the book would reinvigorate the practice for a new generation.

His daughter, Susannah Heschel, writes in the introduction, "Observing the Sabbath is not only about refraining from work, but about creating *menuha*, a restfulness that is also a celebration."[7] *Menuha* is a Hebrew word that refers to the "happiness and contentment that come from experiencing and knowing that things are as they ought to be, and that they are primordially and constitutively good."[8] It conveys a sense that life is a gift that ought to be cherished and celebrated fully. The Sabbath should be something to look forward to, to celebrate as we rest our bodies and souls. And, Susannah Heschel adds, "It is not we who long for a day of rest, but the Sabbath spirit that is lonely and longs for us."[9] It is a beautiful thought that Sabbath longs for us also, that *kairos* time calls out to us to slow down, to be still and notice the world around us.

Abraham Joshua Heschel saw that the Sabbath needed defending from the onslaught of productivity demanded by the industrial-consumer complex of American society and the increasing emphasis on obtaining money and more stuff. "Yet to have more does not mean to be more," he writes. "The power we attain in the world of space terminates abruptly at the borderline of time, but time is the heart of existence."[10]

This casts time in a positive light, as a reminder that we can acquire all the material possessions in the world, but acquisition has no effect on one's quantity of life. Heschel felt that people had sold themselves "into slavery of things" and so had become broken.[11] For him, the antidote was to reclaim a sense of holiness in life, with the Sabbath at its heart.

Judaism places an emphasis on these holy moments—*kairos* moments—as well as holy sites, which have been important to Jewish life and worship across time. Heschel writes, "The mythical mind would expect that, after heaven and earth have been established, God would create a holy place—a holy mountain or a holy spring—whereupon a sanctuary is to be established. Yet is seems as if to the Bible it is *holiness in time*, the Sabbath, which comes first."[12]

After the Second Temple was destroyed by the Romans in 70 CE, Judaism was no longer a religion of a particular place but a religion that could be practiced anywhere by anyone. Instead of the temple, the Sabbath is now the holy place, a time out of time when we reconnect with an ever-present God. In Heschel's words, "The seventh day is a *palace in time* which we build," the "climax of living."[13]

This concept of a "place in time" is important; Heschel doesn't argue that we should or can entirely step out of this technological capitalist system that is the modern world, but he asserts that we take time away from it to renew ourselves and reconnect with God. There is no way, apart from living as a hermit, to remove ourselves from the chaotic, imperfect, tragic world around us. But we can take a break by connecting with the present moment, being still and quiet enough to hear what God might be saying to us.

SOLITARY SABBATH

There are a few specific practices that can help us cultivate these kinds of solitary moments out of chronological time, to step outside the busy flow of our lives and, as Heschel encourages us, "call the Sabbath a delight: a delight to the soul and a delight to the body."[14] While practicing sabbath should give us joy and reinvigorate our lives, I want to recognize that the ability to take time to be still is a luxury not available to everyone. The ability to take a day off from work or to enjoy a regular weekend very much depends on a person's economic status. Many people in our society work every single day, often at two or even three jobs to provide for themselves and their families. An entire day of rest without either work or family obligations may be entirely untenable for you. But Sabbath doesn't have to be an entire day, from one sunset to the next. It can be celebrated for any length of time. Even just meditating for twenty minutes in the morning is a way of stepping out of time to be present in the moment and rest with God.

Over a year ago, in our poetry group discussion, a friend posed a great question about sabbath. He asked if any of us had ever spent an entire day, sunrise to sunset, without doing anything productive—not writing or reading or watching TV, just enjoying being alive. None of us had, but his challenge stayed with me and, one Saturday, I finally decided to try it.

Because my professional life revolves around words, I called it a sabbath from words. I planned to not read or write, to not drive anywhere or buy anything or watch TV, from sunrise to sunset. When I woke up that morning, I ate breakfast and then sat in the backyard, drinking coffee and welcoming the day. After a little while, I took my dog for a walk around the neighborhood, made a second cup of coffee, and sat some more. In the late morning, when my back got sore from sitting, I went into the garden and pulled weeds. I ate lunch, and then went back outside, watching the shadows of the trees move across the grass as the sun moved through the sky above me. I went for another walk, watched the birds—geese flying south in formation and my friend the merlin hunting in the field beyond the fence. I ate dinner and watched the sun set in glorious reds and oranges.

It was a gorgeous day, and I absorbed every bit of it. But inside, my mind was churning, uncomfortable with a lack of stimulation. Throughout the day, I was sad to notice myself getting bored, wanting to be somewhere else other than soaking in the quietness of creation. By the end of the day, though, a deep peace started to settle over me. The whole landscape began to feel like it was breathing slowly, a living being with only the illusion of distinct parts. The squirrel darting across my line of sight seemed to be one with the wild grape vine it was traveling on, a sinuous ropey path. And when a barred owl swooped out of a tree in the distance, I felt my heart skip a beat from the majesty of such a silent sight, a flash of white against the green of the trees. There were moments when it felt like I was in withdrawal from the addictiveness of a busy life, but at other times I felt completely comfortable in my own skin, bare feet sinking into the grass.

I highly recommend this sabbath challenge: try to spend a day not creating, not striving, simply being. If you don't have an entire day to devote, there are countless ways to practice a mini-sabbath. Even spending just half an hour outside in the morning, watching the birds and the branches swaying in the breeze, can be immensely restorative.

I often spend the first and last hour of each day sitting outside unless it's bitterly cold. This time to be still and watch the world around me gives me strength each morning—strength that I can carry into my day—and in the evening it helps me process the events of the day. These are also the times when lots of wildlife are out—deer foraging, squirrels gathering nuts, barred owls calling out. When you stop to watch and listen and share quiet space with these creatures, you may find you cannot help but feel their energy running through your own body.

Meditation is perhaps one of the most easily available sabbath practices for waking up to the present moment. You can do it anywhere, at any time, for any length of time. Simply sit in a chair with your feet flat on the floor and focus on your breath. *In and out. In and out.* You can count your breaths, or you might recite a short phrase or prayer with each breath. When thoughts come into your mind, simply let them pass by without engaging them. If this seems daunting, start with just five minutes a day and work up from there. Sometimes, before I meditate, I will read a passage from the lectionary of the day, but other times I'll just dive right in. It's amazing how quickly this practice can bring you peace during the rest of the day, grounding you in the present moment, even in difficult situations.

Another solitary sabbath practice is simply spending time in the natural world, whether that be a park, a beach, a desert, or a prairie. For most of our evolutionary history until just a few hundred years ago, humans spent most or all their time outside. Hundreds of millions of people who live in rural agricultural communities throughout the world still do spend almost all their time in intimate contact with nature. Many in the industrial West have forgotten the simple fact that our bodies and nervous systems are adapted for close connection to the natural world.

The quickest way to calm myself when I'm feeling upset is simply to walk outside and look up at the sky. Immediately, my heart rate slows, my breathing deepens, and I remember that I am part of the larger landscape. Sitting outdoors or walking slowly outdoors are both excellent ways to connect with the natural world. Walking slowly is different from either going for a hike or a run, because slow walking gives you time to pay close attention to the plants and animals around you, the mourning dove singing from the telephone line, or rows of goldenrod bobbing in the breeze.

Trees and forests seem to have a hold on our imaginations as sacred places of renewal. In Japan there is a tradition called *shinrin-yoku*, or forest bathing, which involves simply spending time in a forest, allowing the presence of trees to calm one's being.[15] This can take the form of walking in the woods, sitting under a tree in a city park, or resting in a hammock. The original practice of *shinrin-yoku* was based on "walking through the forest at a gentle pace for two hours or more," exemplified by the Japanese phrase *shikan shouyou* which means "nothing but wandering along."[16]

Forest bathing places a premium on paying attention to the present moment, to sights, smells, and sounds in the trees around you, as well as paying attention to how your body feels as you move through the forest. Part of this practice can include touching trees, feeling the roughness of the bark on your fingers, and even sitting for a period of silent meditation in a forest setting, centering your awareness and grounding yourself in the landscape.

I recently learned of a similar practice: the act of beholding trees, which means taking the time to sit or stand and pay attention to a single tree for an extended period.[17] The idea is to see the tree as a whole being, and as a part of the mesh-work landscape around it. Trees are connected to one another underground by their root systems, which are interwoven with fungal networks. Above ground, trees communicate with one another by emitting pheromones and other chemicals that are passed from tree to tree on the wind. No one tree lives in isolation. There is much beauty to behold when we stand or sit next to a tree.

I practiced this recently on a trip to a friend's farm outside of the city—it's forty-five acres of fruit orchards, hay fields, and forests, some of which are quite old. There is a particular spot on her property where I like to camp, next to an intermittent stream nestled between two hills.

After I set up my tent, I sat down next to a large walnut tree I've always been particularly fond of. It is probably a hundred feet tall, and the trunk branches into two, fairly close to the ground. The notch where the trunk branches has rotted and is now soil for a tuft of grass and several different species of wildflowers that resemble a head of green hair on the old tree.

I sat for half an hour beholding this tree in all its quiet grandeur, as the dappled light danced on its trunk and its branches swayed high above me in the breeze, bright green against a deep blue autumn sky. I found myself thinking about the part of the tree that is unseen, all the roots that spread out under the ground, anchoring it to that spot. I wondered how deep the roots went, and how wide they were spread; when we look at a tree, we're only ever seeing half of its form. At the end of the time, I slowly walked up to it and put my hands on the bark. It felt cold and rough but strangely reassuring, like an old friend. I found myself filled with wonder at this one particular manifestation of creation, growing quietly beyond my lifetime, by a stream, in a cleft of hills in rural Ohio.

COMMUNITY SABBATH

In addition to celebrating a sabbath in a solitary way, communal sabbath practices are also crucial in helping us step out of chronological time and slow down together. As Heschel observes, "The Sabbath itself is a sanctuary which we build, *a sanctuary in time*,"[18] and something that we can build together in community.

For over ten years I attended unprogrammed Quaker meetings in several cities where I lived. I discovered that there is nothing more sacred and nourishing than sitting quietly with a group of people for an hour, listening for the voice of God speaking to us communally. To this day, when I walk into a Quaker meeting, I immediately feel myself becoming calmer and more attentive. But if sitting in silence for an hour doesn't sound appealing, there are plenty of other ways to practice sabbath in a community.

Among the favorite offerings of my church's creation care group are monthly nature walks, open to folks of all ages who want to connect with God through the natural world. Some people come because they love watching birds, others come to learn something new about nature, and I suspect many of the younger participants come to hang out with their friends. But no matter the personal motivation, the experience is nourishing, because it helps us connect, together, with the beauty and joy present in the natural world. Even in the chilly weather of midwinter, there are always interesting things to see, and being able to share these sights and sounds with friends makes the experience even more meaningful.

The leader of the nature walk opens with a prayer or short devotional and reminds the group that in order to see all of what nature has to offer, we should keep talking to a minimum and focus on listening to the plants and animals around us. This is no mere walk in the woods with friends, but a sacred time for observing the presence of God in the landscape through which we move.

Worshiping outdoors is another ancient practice that is gaining new life in the form of wild churches, also called forest churches. Most of Jesus' ministry happened in open outdoor spaces: on mountainsides, on wide plains, or on lakeshores. The early Anabaptists often met in forests and caves to elude authorities as they worshiped in secret. The Forest Church movement in the United Kingdom started around 2012 and has dozens of communities that regularly worship in parks or other open lands.[19] The Wild Church Network was started in North America by Wendy Janzen, Victoria Loorz, and a few others in 2016, with six worshiping groups, and as of 2022 had well over 100 groups.

Janzen likens the Network's growth to that of the early Anabaptist movement, which was characterized by geographically scattered groups with similar beliefs starting worshiping communities alone and then networking with one another. These groups throughout the United States and Canada have been forming to worship outside because they feel called outdoors to reconnect worship with their particular places.[20] This reconnection is more pertinent than ever as we become aware of our dependence on the earth for sustenance and as we deal with climate change threats to the precarious balance of local ecosystems.

Wendy Janzen was moved to start the Burning Bush Forest Church in Kitchener, Ontario, in 2014, after conversations with a neighbor who confided in her that she was done with formal church, tired of sitting inside a building while people talked at her. She told Janzen she would much rather spend her time hiking with her family, because that was where she felt most connected to God. The neighbor indicated that she would like to do this with other families, especially if it was "something more" than just hiking.

Janzen says, "I felt there was something significant about this conversation that I needed to pay attention to. Then when I was picking up my son from forest school, it was like an epiphany—could there be such a thing as forest church? Could that be what the conversation with my neighbor was pointing us toward?"[21]

She started doing research and found the newly formed Forest Church Network in the United Kingdom, which was formed out of a small group of congregations who were worshiping outdoors throughout Britain. Her realization that there were already communities worshiping outdoors motivated her to start her own congregation. Burning Bush Forest Church now gathers twice a month, all year long, in public parks in Kitchener, with a group of 15 to 25 people. There is always at least one first-time visitor, often several, and the group is diverse, including those who participate in other congregations in a variety of denominations, those who have given up church attendance, and those who grew up not attending church. The congregation is guided by the principle that church isn't just a place where you sit and listen to someone talking; it's dynamic, involving both the human and the nonhuman community.[22]

As with other wild churches, each service at Burning Bush involves four basic elements: Gathering and Grounding, Reading and Reflecting, Wandering and Wondering, and Sharing and Sending. The Gathering and Grounding portion of the service includes a welcome, a land acknowledgment, and a meditation for bringing the congregation into awareness of where they are gathered. During this time, they address the community of creation, greeting the sky and trees and earth; they check in with what they feel through each of their senses—listening, smelling, and embodied awareness. This is followed by a prayer of invocation.

During the Reading and Reflecting portion of the service, they listen to scripture readings, poetry, quotes, and a short reflection that is meant to give some seeds for contemplation during the next portion. Following this is thirty minutes of Wandering and Wondering time, when congregants explore the location, with the goal of listening for where the voice of God might be speaking to them at the moment. They then come back together for a period of communal reflection on what people encountered during their quiet exploration time.

The service sometimes includes communion or candle lighting during Advent, and other rituals throughout the year. It ends with a sending blessing.[23]

This mode of worship—outdoors, surrounded and permeated by the natural world—feels much closer to how Jesus went about his ministry than a traditional church service in a sanctuary. It reflects the reality that, as Janzen puts it, "church isn't a place where you sit and listen to someone talking. It's dynamic."[24] Wild church involves not just the human community, but the biotic community as well; every living organism is present in the act of worship when it is not confined by walls and a roof. Burning Bush meets in all seasons of the year, even in rain, snow, and the early darkness of winter. It is easy to worship outdoors when the weather is sunny and pleasant, but there is something powerful and deep about listening for the voice of God in the wetness of a rainy day, with drops pattering down on your head and feet sloshing through puddles.

I recently had my own experiment with wild church, during our annual church retreat at a camp in central Ohio. My colleague Mark Rupp and I planned an outdoor service modeled after the same plan described above. We imagined that it would be a typically gorgeous fall day, crisp but not cold, and full of sunshine, an easy setting for appreciating the beautiful bounty of creation.

The weather had other plans, however. That whole weekend, low clouds blocked all sunshine, and the wind howled as the outer remnants of Hurricane Ian passed nearby. On Sunday morning, we decided to proceed with meeting outdoors, but participants were all huddled in blankets against a fierce cold wind. We kept the speaking portion as brief as possible, and then dismissed people out onto the grounds to experience the presence of God and to bring back something from nature to decorate the altar for the celebration of communion.

In the end, the service went well despite the cold wind, and several participants shared afterward how meaningful it had been to walk around with the intention of worship. It allowed them to see the landscape in a new light—the rustling of the grass, the hawk soaring high above, the bite of the wind on a bare cheek. One person said that he felt, for the first time, how the act of work and of moving his body was also an act of worship, which he noted is a common teaching in the Amish community. Another person noticed that, when she sat in the tall grass, the wind dissipated, and the air felt much warmer close to the earth.

Everyone came back with beautiful items for the altar, wildflowers of all sorts—asters, goldenrod, and white snakeroot; leaves in various states of color change; acorns, hickory nuts, and buckeyes. One child decorated the whole edge around the altar with lichen-covered bark from the ground nearby. That whole morning, I kept thinking about the early Anabaptists, who met in places like this, out in the wild, to avoid the eyes of the authorities. They too must have been cold on windswept hills or in the middle of winter.

Worshiping outside is an embodied practice that involves our whole being. This practice provides us with the opportunity to connect to the natural world, rather than simply talk about it in the comfort of an air-conditioned building. In Janzen's words, wild church "taps into that sense of awe and wonder that so many of us are missing in our lives."[25] Connecting to God, one another, and the more than human world surrounding us through wild church involves all of who we are—our bodies, our hearts, and our creative minds. This is a mode of doing church that appears to be resonating with diverse groups of people, as new outdoor worshiping communities are popping up all over the world.

PUTTING IT INTO PRACTICE: MAKING TIME FOR SABBATH
There are many ways to slow down and loosen our grip on chronological time as we reconnect with God and the

community of creation. Often, these practices are about doing less rather than taking something else on. To sit in meditation is to wake up to the present moment and remember our embodied reality. Walking contemplatively through a field or forest does the same thing. And these practices do more than simply benefit our emotional lives; they are also good for the earth. Spending time sitting in your backyard or on a rooftop garden requires no burning of fossil fuels or consumption of resources.

We often think of climate advocacy or environmental work as something we need to *do*, to take on, but slowing down and doing less is sometimes better.[26] Learning to listen to the voice of God speaking during a wild church service or a birding hike is just as valuable—these listening practices remind us that we are whole, and they help us to be content in who we are.

One of the most important ways to begin orienting our lives toward sabbath is to carve out a regular time to take a break. Whether it is one day or afternoon each week or a regular daily time for a shorter sabbath, getting into a routine is helpful for maintaining a practice of resting. Pick a time of day or week when you can reliably spend time by yourself or in a group, being still. In seasons or climates where the weather is mild, being out in nature can amplify the feeling of connecting with God, but it isn't a requirement. In the summer, I often spend my first and last hour of the day sitting in my backyard, but in the winter, I make it a point to watch the sunset every evening from my window, even if it's obscured by clouds. Just taking a few minutes to sit and point my body in the direction of the setting sun grounds me in the present moment, helping me to be thankful for my life in the midst of housework or editing or answering emails.

Here are some ideas for you:

1. Start by setting aside a particular time for your sab-
    bath practice. It could be for half an hour each day
    or several hours one day a week. The important thing
    is to be consistent, so it develops into a habit.

2. Decide what sabbath practice most speaks to you. Do
    you enjoy walking reflectively through your neigh-
    borhood or a nearby park? Or, would you rather sit
    quietly under a tree or in a field? If you want to prac-
    tice sabbath with a group of people, consider setting
    aside a time each week to pray or sit quietly together.
    If there is a wild church in your area, think about
    becoming a part of that group's regular worship.

3. Give yourself some grace, if you fall short of your
    goal. Sometimes life gets in the way of even our best
    intentions. If you miss an allotted sabbath time,
    resolve to make space for it the next day or week.
    If you find yourself getting bored with one practice,
    try something different. Your practice might change
    as the seasons change and spending time outside
    becomes more difficult.

Chapter 7

A NEW HEAVEN
AND A NEW EARTH

Climate Justice and Restoring Creation

Then the angel showed me the river of the water of life, bright as crystal, flowing from the throne of God and of the Lamb through the middle of the street of the city. On either side of the river is the tree of life with its twelve kinds of fruit, producing its fruit each month; and the leaves of the tree are for the healing of the nations. (Revelation 22:1–2)

The book of Revelation, bewildering as it is with strange imagery and otherworldly signs, is above all a vision of the restored kin-dom of God. John was writing during the height of Roman persecution, and he dreamed up a future of hope—a place where God will dwell among people, on a renewed earth. This act of imagining a new world and getting to work building it is the final, essential piece of this exploration of what it means to live well on a fragile planet.

The previous two chapters discussed how we can ground ourselves in our local landscapes and how we can take time to reconnect with God and the natural world. This chapter focuses on how we can live well in our communities as we confront environmental racism and climate justice near and far. The world is currently experiencing a climate change revolution, and deep and lasting change cannot come from big governments alone; it also requires millions of communities working on a local level to repair the earth.

We are living in something of a watershed moment when it comes to climate change awareness and action. As I write this, the Unites States Congress has recently passed sweeping climate legislation called the Inflation Reduction Act, that will reduce greenhouse gas emissions by 40 percent by 2030. It includes the most extensive and ambitious tax credits and support for clean energy and the limiting of fossil fuel use that has ever been proposed. The act doesn't call for the 50 percent reduction in emissions that is needed, but it is undeniably a huge step forward, and one that was not expected to pass in such a contentious political climate.

The prices of solar panels and wind turbines have been declining precipitously as their adoption and use have skyrocketed. Energy use from these kinds of renewable sources has increased 90 percent since 2000, and 42 percent since 2010, and it now makes up 20 percent of the total power generation of utilities in the United States.[1] Electric vehicles have entered the mainstream, making up 10 percent of new car sales globally in 2021, with a 75 percent increase in the first half of 2022 alone.[2] When I turn on the television, almost every car ad I see is for an electric vehicle of some kind. Contrast this with just twenty years ago, when hybrid vehicles were just starting to emerge on the market for those who could afford them, and electric vehicles were nowhere to be seen except perhaps in testing labs.

While there is significant work to be done and government promises aren't the same as concrete results, the world is in a profound time of change when it comes to confronting climate change and shifting to renewable sources of energy.

But big government actions, while they get the most press, aren't enough to enact the deep and lasting changes in behavior and attitude that are needed to right the sinking ship of our looming environmental catastrophe. This is where the work of local communities comes to the fore, from neighborhood projects to social media activists and local ecological restoration volunteers. These small, people-powered initiatives are helping to shift our culture, to bring about a climate revolution. These countless individuals don't do this work only out of moral obligation or duty to the earth, but because it makes them feel more alive and connected to the people and the landscape around them.

Advertising agencies and corporations would have us believe that the fulfillment of all our desires comes from buying certain things, but the truth is that consumption only leaves people feeling emptier, like food that does not satisfy. Connecting with others around us—in our neighborhood, rural area, or city—grounds us in those places and binds us together with common goals. There is nothing like spending a day handing out boxes of food to hungry neighbors to make me feel connected to my community and grateful for what we all have together. Giving in this way is also a reminder that our society is deeply fractured, when those working multiple jobs still don't make enough money to feed their families. Living well on our fragile planet requires us to extend this connection we develop with the earth, with our bodies, and with God— beyond ourselves into these hopeful acts of restoration.

CREATION AND RE-CREATION IN REVELATION

Although people have been making incorrect predictions about the end of the world based on the prophetic language in Revelation for thousands of years, the book's cataclysmic images feel oddly relevant to our current age, plagued as we are by violence and systemic injustice. The perils of climate change add a layer of urgency, as the world's population faces seemingly apocalyptic floods, wildfires, and hurricanes with increasing frequency and intensity each year. But the book of Revelation has also been used to minimize the need for creation care and climate action. If the earth is going to end, the argument goes, there is nothing we can do to stop it and perhaps we even ought to get out of the way and hasten Jesus' return. So, what are we to do with the book of Revelation? How can it shape our understanding of what it means to live well on our fragile planet?

The book of Revelation, also known as the Apocalypse of John, is an ancient vision of what can emerge from a time of profound turbulence and change—an apocalyptic vision of the downfall of the Roman Empire and the return of a just society. It is also potentially one of the most confusing and misinterpreted books in the Bible. Often quoted in conspiracy theories about the end of days and used as a justification for the total abandonment of a good life on earth in favor of eternal life in heaven, Revelation is in fact a critique of powerful earthly governments. The vision centers the earth as the site of a redeemed creation—the new heavens and new earth will be here, not on some ethereal plane. Reading the book in this way helps us make sense of the language used to describe how the earth speaks and how natural elements have angelic legal representation as persons in the heavenly court.

It is easy for us in our hyper-modern mindset to dismiss this language as mere metaphor, but that is a serious misreading of the text. Revelation and other apocalyptic literature, including the Old Testament books of Daniel and Ezekiel, make it clear that natural and spiritual powers are bound up inextricably with one another. New Testament scholar Barbara Rossing argues that not only do natural features have spiritual powers, "systems of oppression and empire also have a corporate spirit" that is described as a beast or demon.[3] It is the structural nature of these powers that makes them so destructive, and apocalyptic literature like Revelation can be understood as a vision for how to dismantle these empires built on violence and injustice. Revelation offers a vision of hope that provides strength for resisting, even when success seems impossible.

Empires and totalitarian regimes will harness language and logic to legitimize their oppression, and apocalyptic literature seeks "to answer that logic by galvanizing people's imagination for resistance."[4] In the case of Revelation, that answer comes in the vision of a new heaven and new earth, restored to harmony. In Revelation 21–22, the very last chapters of the Bible, John details an alternative vision of reality after the fall of earthly empires. Notably, it is not humans who are taken up to some ethereal plane of existence, but the new city of Jerusalem that comes down to earth (21:2). This renewed earthly city becomes the dwelling place of God (21:3) and living water is given freely to all (21:6). Likewise, the tree of life that grows beside the river of life provides fruit free to all (22:2). The economy of gift—where the bounty of the natural world is available to all without cost—is the opposite of the force of empires.

No matter how impossible this vision may seem, the liberation and restoration that John describes and the downfall of exploitive forces that he predicts offer us a picture of hope, of something worth living into. The restored earth is a place where all people are fed from the bounty of the tree of life, where all have enough, and no one hoards wealth for themselves. With this future hope in the forefront of our minds, we can find many ways to live into this vision of restored shalom in our own communities, here and now, even amidst the ongoing reality of injustice.

FINDING OUR PLACE: LOCAL RESOURCES FOR LOCAL COMMUNITIES

The previous chapters have explored the importance of reclaiming a sense of place, of grounding ourselves in our own landscapes. A crucial part of the biblical ideal of shalom is learning to live well in our local environment. So how can we do this in our own local context?

The Transition Town movement offers one model for how local communities can try to reinhabit their local places. This movement, started in Totnes, Devon, in England, is so named because the movement's goal is to help communities transition away from reliance on fossil fuels and imported goods to the use of sustainable energy and goods that are produced locally. The people of the town wanted to make their own community more resilient in the face of climate-change-induced disruptions to the supply chain. They seek to do this by sourcing food, fuel, and other goods from the local area instead of importing these things from other nations. Though the work is ongoing, they have instituted a variety of projects related to growing food locally, helping neighbors build relationships with one another, and working to insulate and sustainably power the homes in the town.[5] This movement has since spread all over the world, and it has taken on new urgency, given the supply-chain woes caused by the pandemic that continue to affect daily life.

Transition Towns are based on the idea that participation is crucial for building a connected community and that every person has a role to play in helping a community become more resource-independent. Positive change won't just happen without us.

Environmental ethicist Michael Northcott in *Place, Ecology and the Sacred* notes, "The core political assumption of Transition is that *participation* in creating community is essential to the recovery of a local economy, where people are again engaged in meeting their own needs for food, shelter, entertainment and personal care, instead of relying on large corporations and government agencies."[6] The Transition movement engages people as "subjects rather than objects of change."[7] It's not a top-down government approach, but a bottom-up community-centered approach.

There are now Transition groups on every continent except Antarctica and in many American states. The Transition Network, a UK-based nonprofit, keeps data on independent Transition communities. You can search a map on the organization's website to see if there is a Transition Town in your area.[8] Transition groups can be big or small, incorporating an entire town in the case of Totnes, or a small urban neighborhood in the midst of a city. A search for my local area turned up five Transition groups in Ohio and four in Indiana. There is a Transition group in northwest Indiana that formed in 2020 to advocate for the safe closure of a nearby coal-fired power plant and the removal of toxic coal ash waste. They have now branched out to tackle other environmental issues in their area with an emphasis on building solidarity among all affected groups in their communities.[9]

These organic communities are arising all over the world, driven by small groups of people who want to grow in place, to put down roots and care for their neighbors and their local landscapes. Northcott notes that "Transition Towns represents a genuine and hopeful attempt to relocalise political economy in order to bring human consumption and exchange activities back into sustainable scale to the capacities of local ecosystems to support them."[10] While most of these groups are small, with limited scope and influence, many seemingly tiny initiatives add up to a big impact on making the earth a more habitable place.

Establishing Transition Towns can help us reclaim a deeper sense of dwelling in our unique communities, a mode of living that strengthens our ties to those places. And this connects us more deeply to our faith and biblical roots, as well. Northcott argues that many Europeans and North Americans have lost the idea that their places have a sacred genealogy. He goes on to say that "the recovery of that genealogy using the dominant religion of these nations, which is Christianity, is a powerful source of redemption and repair to the pathologies of extreme mobility, placelessness and ecological destruction that characterize contemporary life."[11]

The Christian vision of the kin-dom of God and the gift economy promoted by Jesus offer a way to live well with the other life-forms on our planet, and they strengthen us to invest in the well-being of our local communities. This is in stark contrast to the approach of the capitalist system, which places a premium on mobility, expecting workers to be plugged in wherever is most efficient for corporations, and preventing workers from establishing roots in a particular community.

Often people jump at the chance to transfer to a different geographic location for a job believing that staying in the same place is equal to failure. We are taught that we should always be seeking to "move up" in the world, doing whatever it takes to make that happen. Young adults who grow up in rural areas often leave for cities that have better employment opportunities, depriving their home areas of a new generation. This mobility hurts rural economies and societies and causes them to decline even more as depopulation escalates. Moving away from extended family and other social support networks leaves people vulnerable, having to rely only on themselves or their immediate families. Frequent relocation only compounds this problem, as people don't have time to develop any deep community connections before moving on to the next place.

There is no simple antidote to this problem, but individuals and families can develop deeper roots in a community by committing to staying in a particular place. It requires a reframing of how we think about what it means to live well on our fragile planet. Northcott coined the term "parochial ecology" to represent "a morally and ecologically viable alternative to the placeless drift of the global market." He writes that "this would also go some way to repair the relational and spiritual deficit of the individualism and loneliness that the market-based societies of strangers promote."[12]

Transition Towns are a tangible example of this commitment to place and the community we build together when we emphasize rootedness rather than mobility. We too flourish when we commit ourselves to becoming grounded in our local communities by establishing relationships and working to make our neighborhoods and cities more livable for everyone. Rooting ourselves in our local places can give us a lifetime of nourishing friendships with others, a more intimate knowledge of the land, and compassion for those who share our ecosystem with us.

EMBRACING OUR ROLE IN ECOLOGICAL RESTORATION

Another way we can reclaim rootedness to our local places is by working to restore the landscapes around us, whether they are urban, rural, or in between. This often means seeking creative solutions to the problems our communities face.

As in many municipalities in the United States, the stormwater in my neighborhood drains into the sewer system rather than into a separate stormwater system. This means that when there is a heavy rainfall—which is becoming increasingly common in the Midwest—the sewer system is easily overwhelmed with rainwater, causing release outlets to overflow into nearby streams and rivers. Rather than build a new stormwater system, the neighborhood has instead opted to build a system of stormwater runoff mitigation, where rain is trapped in a series of small ponds so it can soak back into the soil, rather than filling up the sewers with clean water. The city has built a network of these ponds along hilly streets and planted water-loving plants in them. City streets have become an interconnected web of tiny urban gardens that keep the rain on the land where it falls.

There were worries about the viability of the project and about it attracting mosquitoes, but I have yet to smell sewage when I walk along the stream even after the heaviest rainstorms, and neighbors have not noticed an increase in mosquitoes. This is an example of ecological restoration in an urban environment, an effort that makes the landscape better for biodiversity and a more beautiful place.

We may think that ecological restoration is primarily the preservation of wilderness areas—absent of humans, where the rest of nature can thrive without us. But living well on this fragile planet requires an expanded imagination to include the environments in which we live our daily lives. Putting our focus on fixing "somewhere else" negates the fact that humans are part of nature, sentient animals who inhabit almost every part of the planet. Before the establishment of the great national parks, countless Indigenous nations lived, hunted, and farmed on those lands. The idea of a wilderness devoid of humans is a modern creation, born out of our notions that humans are separate from the rest of the natural world. Even the embrace of the wilderness as a therapeutic retreat from our urban environments only furthers this nature/culture split. In Northcott's words, "while fetishizing the wild, wilderness as therapy fails to deal with the larger social, political and economic issues that lie at the root of the alienation between urban industrial civilisation and the earth."[13] We must find a way to reintegrate nature and culture if we truly want to live well, the way we were meant to live.

Scripture presents a vision of a restored and healed creation. In the Bible, visions of ecological restoration focus not on a wilderness in a pristine, human-free state, but as "the place for a new harmony between human habitation and wild species, while the rapacious and oppressive city collapses."[14] This is evidenced in passages such as Isaiah 32:14–17 and Psalm 107:33–37. Verse 14 of Isaiah 32 says: "For the palace will be forsaken, the populous city deserted," while "justice will dwell in the wilderness, and righteousness abide in the fruitful field" (v. 16). In the Bible there is a delineation between wilderness, field, and city, but each of these places is a site of restoration, and all these places are the natural habitat of humans.

Wilderness can, indeed, be a place of retreat, where humans are scarce, but it's important that we not confuse nature with wilderness. In the Bible, the wilderness is a place of retreat, rest, and renewal for the difficult work of justice. Moses, Elijah, John the Baptist, and Jesus all ventured out to the wilderness to gain strength during trying times.

The early monastics, the Desert Fathers and Mothers, also retreated to the wilderness, seeking to devote their lives to prayer. As we seek to follow their examples, it's important to have a balance—preserving wild areas, yes, but also recognizing that some, or all, of these places were once, or are now, inhabited by rural communities of people with their own needs for sustenance and survival.

In the Bible, the narrative arc from the garden of Eden to the story of Joseph can be understood as a cautionary tale about the dangers of large-scale agriculture, with the worldly powers creating wealth for a few, while leaving many impoverished.[15] The garden of Eden was a sort of permaculture farm, providing for all of the needs of Adam and Eve without toil, only gentle tending. The problem for the biblical authors was the scaling up of agriculture to industrial scale, which required slave labor and only enriched the ruling elite, who gathered the plenty into storehouses while their own people starved.

We are living now in a similar cultural moment. Most of the world's monetary wealth is concentrated in the hands of less than one percent of the population. In the United States, a highly developed country with more than enough resources to feed its population, 34 million people live in food insecure households.[16] A full 10 percent of the population routinely does not have enough to eat, in one of the wealthiest nations in the world. In Canada 15.9 percent of households experienced food insecurity in 2021.[17]

As we seek to live well in this reality, we can look to the Bible's perspective that a restoration of the world also involves the undoing of this kind of injustice. The new creation envisioned in Revelation is one where all are fed in the city of God and where water runs freely—neither food nor water are a commodity to be traded.

In the communitarian ethic we find the best framework for understanding this pursuit of the biblical vision of a restored creation that reflects our own environments and pursues justice for the marginalized. Contrary to our dominant social contract, where each person is an autonomous individual who is responsible for meeting their own needs, communitarians recognize that we are all intertwined in a vast web of relationships. We are never separate, independent people, but part of the human and biotic community. By rooting ourselves more deeply in our local places, we are motivated to work for ecological restoration right where we are.

ENVIRONMENTAL JUSTICE IN THE LOCAL SETTING

What can we do in our local communities to restore their ecosystems as well as work for justice for our human neighbors? A good first step is to look for organizations already working for change in your area and to join in the work they are doing. For example, in Chelsea, a suburb of Boston, a local environmental group called GreenRoots started the "Cool Block project" to mitigate the heat island effects of the city's many paved surfaces.

The heat island effect happens when dark, hard surfaces like roofs, sidewalks, and parking lots absorb the heat of the sun and then warm the air above them. Heat islands are often found in poor neighborhoods with few trees and little green space, and they can raise the ambient temperature as much as seven degrees above the temperature of greener areas.[18]

For the project in Chelsea, neighbors have chosen one city block where there was virtually no green space, and they have planted almost fifty trees, ripping up the sidewalks to install planters and porous concrete paving stones. They are also painting the dark asphalt gray, a color that which reflects heat instead of absorbing it. They are negotiating with the local Boys & Girls Club to install a white roof, which would also reflect heat.[19]

All these seemingly small changes add up when it comes to mitigating the effects of the sweltering summer heat. The group has plans to pay residents to water the trees, ensuring their long-term survival, and to measure the success of the project, researchers from Boston University plan to track the ambient temperature as well as 911 calls about heat-related distress.

In my own city, a social justice organization called BREAD recently began a climate justice campaign. The organization started the process by requesting input from city residents about how environmental pollution affects them, and heat islands were a leading topic of conversation here, too. BREAD chose to sponsor legislation in the city council to create a tree ordinance that would prevent trees from being cut down without cause and therefore protecting the existing green space in the city. Trees, especially mature ones, are excellent at mitigating heat, offering cool shade for people and pavement alike.

Heat islands aren't the only environmental issue we face. As noted above the city has an old sewer infrastructure that collects not only sewage but also all stormwater runoff from roadways, which easily overwhelms the system in heavy rain. In 2010, my home congregation, Columbus Mennonite Church, installed a rain garden, in partnership with Friends of the Lower Olentangy Watershed (FLOW) to show how even one building can make an impact on stormwater runoff. A rain barrel collects water from one side of the building, while water from the other side of the building is funneled into the rain garden that contains plants that thrive in wet environments. These plants soak up the water as it falls, preventing it from becoming storm runoff and easing the pressure on the aging sewer system.

This small project doesn't make a big dent in the amount of stormwater runoff flowing into the sewer system, but it does serve as "demonstration project evangelism," to use Ched Myers's words, pointing a way forward to other households or businesses that want to become more environmentally friendly.[20] The rain garden predated the large stormwater run-off project I described earlier, and I wonder whether the rain garden was the inspiration for the stormwater project.

Stormwater runoff might not sound to you like an issue of justice. However, the runoff of raw sewage and toxic waste affects not only the fragile ecosystem of the river but also the people who rely on fish from the river for needed food. Poor people in many cities rely on fish to supplement their meager food budget, and runoff puts them at risk for disease caused by toxic discharges from industry as well as sewage.

Another local example of environmental justice is the ubiquitous and humble farmers market. While farmers markets have sprung up in almost every county in the United States, it's easy to overlook their significance for confronting environmental injustice. Farmers markets connect farmers directly to consumers, providing a tangible link to sources of food and the people who grow it. Farmers who sell their products at markets make more money than when selling to wholesale distributors, so their income gets a boost.

When you shop at a farmers market, you are supporting local businesses and making a connection to your food that you simply can't by perusing the aisles of a grocery store. When I buy lettuce, kale, bok choy, and other greens (some of my favorite veggies) at the local farmers market, I have a chance to chat with the people who grew the food I so love to eat. They often offer me tips about cooking some of the stranger vegetables, and they tell me what will be in season each week. This enables me to be more connected to the agricultural seasons of my region and to the mostly rural communities responsible for the nation's food supply.

Many farmers markets in the U.S. offer programs for food assistance, so that food stamp recipients can convert their credits into tokens to redeem for fresh produce, often at a discounted rate. The United States Department of Agriculture website even has a farmers market search program, where recipients can find a market that accepts their benefits.

Compared to processed food, fresh produce can be prohibitively expensive for food-insecure families. A box of macaroni and cheese costs the same as a head of broccoli, and though the pasta provides more calories and protein that will make their family feel full, it has a much lower nutritional value than the fresh vegetable. With limited funds, people are forced to choose between providing enough food and providing quality food for their families. Farmers market programs offer affordable options and promote food justice in the process.

Farmers markets are also a great location for getting to know your neighbors better. Markets are natural places for people in the local community to congregate and to share stories. I have a friend in rural Georgia who became deeply involved in immigrant justice simply by talking with his neighbors, who were primarily migrant farmworkers. He listened to their stories and began helping where he could. Chatting with your neighbors seems like such a small kindness, but small actions can grow into something much larger. My friend's whole congregation is now involved, helping their neighbors as well as advocating for political action at the state and national level. Many of my neighbors face food insecurity themselves, something I wouldn't have learned if I hadn't ventured out into my community to see for myself.

A FLOURISHING COMMUNITY

The projects and ideas mentioned in this chapter can, by themselves, seem incredibly small and insignificant in the face of the global catastrophe that climate change is wreaking on our planet. But when even tiny communities of people around the world begin to change their behavior, these small changes add up. And as Christians, we live for more than just results. God calls us to live faithfully, acting to protect and restore the planet not because we can see the outcome, but because this work brings us closer to God and to one another. Becoming grounded in our local places is meaningless unless we are also connected to the human community around us, helping where we can, and accepting help when needed.

The relatively simple premise behind initiatives like these is that connecting with your neighbors, the others in your community whether it is large or small, is the foundation for both confronting injustice and for rooting oneself more deeply in one's local place. Understanding the environmental and social realities in your community is the first step in working toward meaningful change, and that understanding upends the modern illusion of autonomous individualism. One way to redevelop the gift economy that Jesus preached is to delve into the conditions of your community and support those in need. The antidote to the modern breakdown between nature and culture is reconnecting with our places and our local communities. This is a reinvigoration of the economy of gift, where we recognize all we have been given, and we make sure that everyone else also has what they need to flourish.

PUTTING IT INTO PRACTICE: CLIMATE JUSTICE IN YOUR AREA

Though climate change is a thoroughly global problem, you don't have to look far to find places where you can make a difference in addressing it. As mentioned above, a good place to start is to look for organizations in your area who are working to address climate justice issues. Heat islands primarily impact urban low-income communities with little access to green space. Look for social justice organizations or environmental nonprofits that might be working on this and other issues. Industrial pollution is another driver of climate change as well as a cause of health problems in the communities that surround the pollution source. People of color are disproportionately affected by industrial pollution. If you live in the U.S., check out the excellent website of the NAACP for resources for addressing this issue as well as opportunities to get involved in ecojustice projects throughout the country.[21]

If you want to begin with your own family's contribution to climate change, you can start by learning about your carbon footprint. A carbon footprint is a measurement of how much carbon dioxide a household produces in a year, based on calculations that take into account how much you drive, what you eat, how often you fly, and other factors. Residents of the U.S. can calculate their carbon footprint on the website of the Environmental Protection Agency and can find tips for beginning to reduce one's carbon impact on the planet.[22]

Here are some things to consider:

1. Take a tour of your town or city. What do you see? Are there neighborhoods that are close to industrial sites or that have little or no tree cover?

2. What resources are available to you in your local area? Are there organizations or groups you can join that are already working on climate justice issues?

3. If you want to start with your own household, do a carbon footprint calculation test. Think about what you might do to lessen your carbon footprint, such as cycling to work or church, walking instead of driving if you are running an errand that is close by, or taking a train instead of flying.

CONCLUSION

Returning to Wonder

When they had heard the king, they set out; and there, ahead of them, went the star that they had seen at its rising, until it stopped over the place where the child was. When they saw that the star had stopped, they were overwhelmed with joy. On entering the house, they saw the child with Mary his mother; and they knelt down and paid him homage. Then, opening their treasure chests, they offered him gifts of gold, frankincense, and myrrh. (Matthew 2:9–11)

In the process of writing this book, I decided to practice what I was preaching and engage in something tangible in my community. This led to the formation of the Olentangy Wild Church, a small group of folks from my congregation and the local community who have started worshiping once a month in a local park.

For most of my life, I have lived primarily in my mind, in a refuge of words that I share with the world indirectly through my writing. Starting a worshiping community was not something I envisioned doing as I approached my fortieth birthday, but I have felt a strong and persistent call to share my love of the spiritual aspects of the natural world with others who are also searching for this same deep connection.

Our first gathering for worship was the Sunday after Thanksgiving, a blustery, rainy day with low gray clouds moving fast overhead. Thankfully, the rain stopped about an hour before, but the ground was muddy, and I was fairly sure that no one would want to be outside on such a windy day, on a holiday weekend. I set up my chair in a clearing at the edge of the forest and sat down, suddenly awed by the massive trunks of the walnut trees standing near me. A stream, flush with clear water from the recent rain, was babbling a short distance away in the forest. I sat quietly in this majestic place, wondering if I would be worshiping by myself. But, one by one, people started to come. We had a small group, but it wasn't just me alone, and our time together felt incredibly sacred.

We started by reading Romans 8:18–24 from the First Nations Version of the New Testament about the coming redemption of all creation. Then I read a quote from David Abram about how everything breathes—trees, rocks, even beaver ponds. I gave a short reflection on the power of breath and how so often, during the holiday season, we do not take time to be still and breathe, because we're hurrying around— shopping, cooking, attending parties. Advent often feels like a blur of commitments and errands. I told the group that I love to notice how the buds are already on the trees in early winter, waiting through snow and ice for the eventual thaw and arrival of spring. (Making buds is the last act of each tree before it funnels out most of its extra water to prepare for winter storms.) We looked up and saw the red buds already on the maples above our heads, vibrant against the gray sky.

Then we went out for a time of quiet reflection by ourselves. I lay on the cold wet ground, protected only by the thin layer of my raincoat, and I looked at the branches waving in the wind. After ten minutes of looking intently, my vision shifted, and I felt viscerally as if I was looking at blood vessels or lungs in relief, black against a white background. Beautiful. It was such a strange feeling that I had to look away.

When we came back together, each person shared with the group something meaningful about what they had observed during their time alone. They described the wonderful sound of the stream nearby, all the activity of the birds even on this dreary day, and how the flow of water felt like prayer.

I left feeling calm and quiet inside, in a way I haven't felt since I was going to Quaker meeting regularly. Sitting in silence with other people feels particularly sacred, in a way that I don't feel at any other time, including in a church service. It was special to experience that time in nature on such a blustery late fall day, time I would have otherwise spent inside, immune to the beauty around me.

At the beginning of this book, I named two main tensions I feel as a Christian and an environmentalist living on this fragile, beautiful planet. First, the Bible calls us to live differently from what our consumer culture expects. Secondly, the world often feels like a perilous place. I truly believe that the most powerful antidote to climate despair and guilt is to find joy and wonder by doing things like worshiping in the forest. It's important to recognize these feelings of anxiety and despondency; in fact, it's hard to have any deep connection with the natural world without them.

But the path toward climate disaster is not set in stone. When we lose hope, we forget that our actions do matter, for the earth and for the community of beings that surrounds us. Focusing on what is going wrong also blinds us to the beauty seeping out all around, even in the midst of upheaval and destruction. The buds still appear on the tall branches. Flocks of blackbirds wheel overhead in elaborate patterns as they migrate south. The sunset bleeds breathtaking hues of orange and pink across the sky on clear evenings. The world is not doomed but bursting with life.

Worshiping outdoors, going for nature hikes, and writing our own psalms and laments are all ways we can begin to live differently and resist the devastating consumerism and individualism of our culture. My hope is that we as Christians can begin to think differently about our faith as we relearn how to relate to the world as the human animals that we are.

We humans have evolved over millions of years, shaped by our constant interaction with the landscape around us and all its myriad life-forms. The life and teachings of Jesus were shaped as much by his deep embeddedness in the desert landscape of Israel as by the religious and political climate of his time. In many ways, the landscapes we inhabit now are vastly different, with our unprecedented urbanization and explosion of technology. We're also much more aware of how precarious our situation is and how fragile most of the world's bioregions are, and this awareness shapes our own faith and memory in particular ways. This is why it's important to be rooted in both Scripture and in the natural world, as we navigate what it means to live well on this fragile planet.

As soon as religion becomes something set in stone, a codified rubric of instructions for how to live in all times and places, it begins to die. The faith of our ancient religious ancestors and the writings they left behind reflect a culture and worldview that are different from our own. But Scripture offers a window into these premodern cultures, and it also remains alive and open to reinterpretation as human culture changes. The peoples depicted in the Bible lived in close connection to the land

and had a profound recognition of their own dependence on the sustenance offered in each season. When the rains didn't come or hail destroyed the crops, they suffered. When the land provided in abundance, they praised the generosity of a loving God. They knew when each constellation would appear in the sky and when birds migrated through. The seasons had a predictable cycle that is interwoven into our liturgical seasons to this day.

Today, few of us in North American society have such an intimate connection to the land in which we dwell. Our food comes from far-off places, grown by strangers we will never meet. Many of us work indoors, disconnected from the ebb and flow of the seasons. But still God calls out to us, beckoning us to reconnect with the place in which we find ourselves. The Bible offers a template for such a reconnection. The ground beneath our feet is also a guide, welcoming us to settle in and pay attention.

Paying attention to the plight of the natural world comes with a price though, because even the most cursory glance reveals a planet in crisis. Wildfires, deforestation, the violence wrought by war, and the slow rise of sea level all remind us of our peril. Feeling the grief and mourning what has already been lost is just as integral to our journey of reinhabitation as joy and wonder.

Talitha Amadea Aho, a hospital chaplain and former youth pastor at a Presbyterian church in Oakland, California, found herself focusing only on the importance of having hope when talking to the youth of her congregation about the climate crisis. But she eventually realized they need something more than that. In her book *In Deep Waters: Spiritual Care for Young People in a Climate Crisis*, she writes, "The young people in my church have their own spiritual ecosystems, balanced delicately between hope and fear. More than teaching them, my job is to help them tend these ecosystems."[1] Living well isn't always about helping people to have hope—to counter the narrative of despair—but to allow both grief and joy to surface in their own time.

As Aho points out, young people alive today have never lived in a stable world that didn't feel like it was ending. "Climate change has bloomed from a crisis to an all-alarm emergency before their eyes . . . the illusion of stability is a foreign concept to Generation Z (born between 1995 and 2010). They know all too well how a virus can come along and rip the fabric of society to shreds while forests burn and shorelines wash away, leaving human and nonhuman creatures bereft and mourning."[2]

We can no longer hold a naive hope that people will do the right thing if they simply understand the situation, as we have seen those in power repeatedly choose a course of inaction. And this, as Aho describes it, has led to "humanity's sin . . . on full display as the climate crisis pulls the curtain back to show us our selfish greed, systemic racism, and collective apathy."[3]

This brings to mind the pivotal role of lament in the Bible. Though we might feel uncomfortable unleashing the depths of our grief and anger to God, when we do so we step into an established biblical tradition.

When I have been struggling with grief for the planet, I have returned many times to Romans 8:18–27. This passage is a reminder that something bigger is in the process of being born. Verse 19 says, "For the creation waits with eager longing for the revealing of the children of God." And in verse 22 we read, "We know that the whole creation has been groaning in labor pains until now."

There is no doubt that the earth suffers because of human hubris and sin, but Romans hints that something greater is unfolding. It's important to remember that there is a distinct difference between hope and optimism. Optimism is based on an analysis of our situation and a logical conclusion that evidence appears to point in a positive direction. There are certainly some signs of optimism that we have turned a corner in addressing climate change, with the actions of both large governments and millions of small local initiatives. But optimism is inherently fragile, because projects and legislation can fail to make the intended impact.

Hope is much more durable and is not based on mere evidence. Sometimes it seems there is little to be optimistic about in the world, but hope is rooted in a deeper foundation. For Paul, hope is something unseen (Romans 8:24–25), something working in the very fabric of creation. After an impressive image of the Holy Spirit interceding for us "with sighs too deep for words" (v. 26), Paul writes in verse 28, "We know that all things work together for good for those who love God, who are called according to his purpose." Hope in God is what propels us forward, even in difficult circumstances, helping us climb out of our despairing place to see the light and beauty that are also breaking open in the world.

When we have felt the depths of our grief and have lamented alongside God over what has been lost, our hearts can break open, letting in all the joy and wonder for what still remains and abides in the world. There is much to mourn on our planet to be sure, but there are also signs of hope, signs that humans are living into a more just and equitable future. This isn't to say that the future is bound to be rosy and perfect, and for those living in a war zone or under oppressive social systems, all the statistics in the world cannot lessen the suffering they experience. But something pivotal happens when we can sit with our grief long enough to realize that God is present in all times and places, and that, even in the midst of ongoing tragedy, there is beauty and joy and wonder.

VISITING WITH THE WISE MEN

As I am finishing this book, the consumer frenzy of Christmas has passed. Epiphany is fast approaching. Christ is alive among us, a gurgling crying infant just beginning life as the depths of winter freeze the ground and blanket it with snow in these longest nights of the year. It is a quiet time, the perfect moment for an unexpected visit from holy messengers.

When I was growing up, my congregation always had a picnic on the evening of Epiphany, whatever day of the week that happened to be. We gathered at a shelter house at White Rock Lake, a large park in the center of Dallas, to eat fried chicken and assorted potluck dishes, drink lemonade, and visit with the magi.

At some point after dinner, while we were munching on cookies and talking, the wise men would walk in the door, pretending to be lost as they looked for the Christ child. They were dressed in magnificent robes of green, purple, and blue, and I was well into adolescence before I realized they were dads from the congregation, including my own father, dressing up for our benefit. We kids always ran outside to see if we could spot their camels.

The visitors stayed with us for a while, talking to us about the star they were following to find the baby Jesus who had just been born and telling us about prophecies of his future greatness. They ate cookies and drank lemonade, and then were off to continue their quest.

What was so special about this night wasn't the sudden, strange appearance of the magi or the search for their camels, though those were always highlights. It was another chance to see my friends and the extended family of my church community, outside of Sunday morning. We were in a different space, too, along a lakeshore at night, city lights glinting across the water.

As I got older, I came to appreciate this celebration in ordinary time even more. It came in the darkest part of winter, when we had all gone back to school after the Christmas break—a celebration in spite of homework and the concerns of our daily lives. Visiting with the wise men was an in-breaking of holiness, interrupting the week to remind us that Jesus had been born among us and that the wise men were seeking him.

This church tradition is also an example of how the stories of the Bible can come alive among us. Our faith involves our whole lives, not just the activities or building of the church. Holiness and revelation aren't limited to a patch of Judean desert at the turn of the first millennium. They are also found on a weeknight, on a dark lakeshore, in the middle of a city. You and I are surrounded by sacredness in all times and places, and our role as Christians is to foster this kin-dom of heaven on the particular places of earth where we dwell, in whatever way we can.

Together we have glimpsed an alternative biblical vision of human creation from holy chaos, our connection to others, animals and plants alike, and our salvation through the incarnate God, who came to heal us and show us an alternative vision of the good life. The Bible is full of stories of people of faith grounded in their own unique landscapes. The Bible guides us as we seek to live well on this fragile earth and to honor the other inhabitants—both human and nonhuman—with whom we share it. We recognize that all the earth belongs to God. The whole of creation is suffused with holiness; every bacterium and drop of water has its own sacred being.

Christianity, in its biblical roots, is grounded in the earth. Ours is a faith founded on social justice for all, the land included, and our scriptures paint a picture of a universe created by God for its own well-being and flourishing, not only for humanity's needs. We are only whole when we are grounded in an enlivened earth. We can only experience God when we are willing to be part of the beautiful, tragic whole of the cosmos.

The future of the church is in re-grounding its people in this ultimate source of being. The kin-dom of heaven will be on a renewed and whole earth, not a disembodied ethereal heaven. The truth of this is found in the vision of a new earth and new heaven in Revelation. We won't flee up to God; the Creator once again walks in the garden with the created ones.

Living well on our fragile planet means embodying this reality in tangible ways—restoring our land, working for justice for our neighbors, and making choices in our daily lives to live out this vision of shalom. These are the ingredients for a faith rooted in the sacred land that enfolds us in its care; this is the faith that God calls us into, earthy and full of life.

ACKNOWLEDGMENTS

This book is the result of several years of conversations with friends, colleagues, and members of my congregation, Columbus Mennonite Church, about what the Bible has to say to us about our rootedness in the land and our community, and how countercultural this message is in our hyper-individualized, consumer-oriented society. I wanted to write a book that would make some of the ideas floating around in ecotheology circles accessible to the people in my congregation who are searching for ways to connect their love of the earth with their Mennonite faith. I hope this book contributes in a small way to this much larger conversation.

Several generous friends were early readers, and I am grateful for the valuable advice of Janeen Bertsche Johnson, Mark Rupp, Cindy Fath, and Shakita Kabicek.

I am also thankful to have an excellent editor at Herald Press, Laura Leonard, who shepherded my manuscript from its rough first draft to completion. I am also immensely grateful for all the staff at Herald Press for their expertise and for believing in this book when it was still in its early stages.

Lastly, a big thank you to my family for supporting my faith and writing for all these years. I am incredibly grateful to have all of you in my life.

NOTES

INTRODUCTION

1. The word kin-dom is a more inclusive way of imagining the community of God that does not involve a ruler and that reflects the reality that we are all kin to one another on this earth.

2. "#YouthStats: Environment and Climate Change," United Nations Office of the Secretary-General's Envoy on Youth, accessed July 8, 2022, https://www.un.org/youthenvoy/environment-climate-change/.

3. Lauren Sommer, "California Just Ran on 100% Renewable Energy, but Fossil Fuels Aren't Fading Away Yet," *NPR*, May 13, 2022, https://www.npr.org/2022/05/07/1097376890/for-a-brief-moment-calif-fully-powered-itself-with-renewable-energy.

4. Seventy-two percent of all US counties now have at least one farmers market, and half of those accept Supplemental Nutritional Assistance Program (SNAP) benefits. "Growth in the Number of U.S. Farmers Markets Slows in Recent Years," USDA, accessed April 19, 2023, https://www.ers.usda.gov/data-products/charts-of-note/charts-of-note/?topicId=f5a7d42d-5209-47db-abbb-2e2cc3634cde.

5. Mary Oliver, "Wild Geese," in *Dream Work* (New York: The Atlantic Monthly Press, 1986), 14.

CHAPTER 1

1. David Abram, *Becoming Animal: An Earthly Cosmology* (New York: Vintage Books, 2010), 55.

2. Abram, 56.

3. Mark I. Wallace, *When God Was a Bird: Christianity, Animism, and the Re-Enchantment of the World* (New York: Fordham University Press, 2019), 8.

4. An animistic understanding of nonhuman nature is present in many places in the Bible, including Genesis 4; Job 12, 38, 42; Psalm 19, 29, 104; Jeremiah 4; Romans 8; Revelation 4–5.

5. Wallace, *When God Was a Bird*, 6.

6. Wallace, 148.

7. Wallace, 30.

8. Wallace, 91.

9. Wallace, 24.

10. This is documented by Alexander Carmichael in his book of collected prayers and songs *Carmina Gadelica*. Alexander Carmichael, *Carmina Gadelica: Hymns and Incantations* (Edinburgh: Floris Books, 1994).

11. John Philip Newell, *Sacred Earth, Sacred Soul: Celtic Wisdom for Reawakening What Our Souls Know and Healing the World* (New York: HarperOne, 2021), 89.

12. John Philip Newell, *The Book of Creation: An Introduction to Celtic Spirituality* (New York: Paulist Press, 1999), xvi.

13. Newell, *Book of Creation*, 71.

14. Newell, *Sacred Earth,* 89.

15. Robert Van de Weyer, ed., *Letters of Pelagius* (Evesham, UK: Arthur James, 1995), 36.

16. Van de Weyer, 76.

17. Tim Flinders, ed., *John Muir* (Maryknoll, NY: Orbis Books, 2013), 69.

18. Randy Woodley, *Shalom and the Community of Creation: An Indigenous Vision* (Grand Rapids, MI: Eerdmans, 2012), 1055.

19. Woodley, 1116.

20. Woodley, 67.

21. Woodley, 273.

22. Woodley, 322.

23. Woodley, 380.

24. Walter Brueggemann, *Peace: Living Toward a Vision* (St. Louis, MO: Chalice Press, 2001), 15.

25. Woodley, *Shalom*, 639.

26. Woodley, 650.

27. Woodley, 756.

28. Woodley, 769.

29. Newell, *Book of Creation*, 4.

30. Gaétan Chevalier et al., "Earthing: Health Implications of Reconnecting the Human Body to the Earth's Surface Electrons," *Journal of Environmental Public Health*, January 12, 2012, https://www.ncbi.nlm.nih.gov/pmc/articles/PMC3265077/.

CHAPTER 2

1. "Doctrine of Discovery," Cornell Law School Legal Information Institute, accessed August 22, 2022, https://www.law.cornell.edu/wex/doctrine_of_discovery.

2. "Bill Moose Run," FLOW, accessed August 22, 2022, https://wiki.olentangywatershed.org/watersheds/bill-moose-run.

3. Will Koehrsen, "Has Global Violence Declined? A Look at the Data," Towards Data Science, January 5, 2019, https://towardsdatascience.com/has-global-violence-declined-a-look-at-the-data-5af708f47fba.

4. "Decline of Global Extreme Poverty Continues but Has Slowed," World Bank, September 19, 2018, https://www.worldbank.org/en/news/press-release/2018/09/19/decline-of-global-extreme-poverty-continues-but-has-slowed-world-bank.

5. Thomas Carothers and Benjamin Press, "Understanding and Responding to Democratic Backsliding," Carnegie Endowment for International Peace, October 20, 2022, https://carnegieendowment.org/2022/10/20/understanding-and-responding-to-global-democratic-backsliding-pub-88173.

6. Ariana N. Gobaud, et al., "Absolute versus Relative Socioeconomic Disadvantage and Homicide: A Spatial Ecological Case—Control Study of US Zip Codes," *Injury Epidemiology* 9, no. 7 (2022), https://injepijournal.biomedcentral.com/articles/10.1186/s40621-022-00371-z.

7. Jawanza Eric Clark, *Reclaiming Stolen Earth: An Africana Ecotheology* (Maryknoll, NY: Orbis Books, 2022), xv.

8. Clark, 83.

9. Clark, xxiii.

10. Clark, 14.

11. Clark, 29.

12. Clark, 183.

13. Clark, 190.

14. Clark, 191.

15. Clark, 192.

16. Clark, 195.

17. Whitney A. Bauman and Kevin J. O'Brien, *Environmental Ethics and Uncertainty: Wrestling with Wicked Problems* (London: Routledge, 2020), 112.

18. Bauman and O'Brien, 112.

19. Ched Myers, *Watershed Discipleship: Reinhabiting Bioregional Faith and Practice* (Eugene, OR: Cascade Books, 2016), 1.

20. Myers, 2.

21. Myers, 2.

22. Myers, 10.

23. Myers, 6.

24. Myers, 369.

25. Wes Jackson, *Becoming Native to This Place* (Berkley: Counterpoint, 1996).

26. "A Guide to Indigenous Land Acknowledgement," Native Governance Center, October 22, 2019, https://nativegov.org/news/a-guide-to-indigenous-land-acknowledgment/.

27. "Land Acknowledgment Resources," Northwestern University, accessed August 27, 2022, https://www.northwestern.edu/native-american-and-indigenous-peoples/about/land-acknowledgment-resources.html.

28. "Guide to Indigenous Land Acknowledgment."

29. "How's My Waterway?" United States Environmental Protection Agency, accessed May 26, 2023, https://mywaterway.epa.gov/.

30. Ched Myers, personal correspondence, 2015.

CHAPTER 3

1. John A. Beck, *The Basic Bible Atlas: A Fascinating Guide to the Land of the Bible* (Grand Rapids, MI: Baker, 2020), 23.

2. Beck, 26.

3. Beck, 30.

4. Beck, 30.

5. Beck, 31.

6. Beck, 33.

7. Enolyne Lyngdoh, "Reclaiming Mother Earth: A Khasi Indigenous Re-Reading of Psalm 104," in *Decolonizing Ecotheology: Indigenous and Subaltern Challenges*, ed. by S. Lily Mendoza and George Zachariah (Eugene, OR: Pickwick Publications, 2022), 69.

8. Lyngdoh, 79.

9. Mark I. Wallace, *When God Was a Bird: Christianity, Animism, and the Re-Enchantment of the World* (New York: Fordham University Press, 2019), 88.

10. Wallace, 67.

11. Wallace, 62.

12. Wallace, 90.

13. James W. Perkinson, "Jesus-Hokmah as Ba'al-Anat: Transgressing Monotheism for the Sake of Indigenous Justice and Planetary Survival," in *Decolonizing Ecotheology: Indigenous and Subaltern Challenges*, ed. by S. Lily Mendoza and George Zachariah (Eugene, OR: Pickwick Publications, 2022), 32.

14. Perkinson, 34.

15. David Abram, *The Spell of the Sensuous: Perception and Language in a More-Than-Human World* (New York: Vintage Books, 1996), 32–33.

16. Abram, 53.

17. Abram, 202.

18. Andreas Weber, *Matter and Desire: An Erotic Ecology* (White River Junction, VT: Chelsea Green, 2014), 8.

19. Weber, 5.

20. "Geologic Map of North America," USGS, accessed May 26, 2023, https://www.usgs.gov/media/images/geologic-map-north-america.

21. Stefan Bengtson et al., "Three-Dimensional Preservation of Cellular and Subcellular Structures Suggests 1.6 Billion-Year-Old Crown-Group Red Algae," *PLOS Biology*, March 14, 2017, https://journals.plos.org/plosbiology/article?id=10.1371/journal.pbio.2000735.

22. Marnie Chesterton, "The Oldest Living Thing on Earth," BBC, June 12, 2017, https://www.bbc.com/news/science-environment-40224991.

23. "Pneuma," *Oxford Classical Dictionary*, March 7, 2016, https://doi.org/10.1093/acrefore/9780199381135.013.5145.

CHAPTER 4

1. Jennifer S. Lerner, et al., "Emotion and Decision Making," *Annual Review of Psychology* 6 (January 2015), 799.

2. Lerner et. al, 801.

3. Lerner et. al, 802.

4. "Majority of US Adults Believe Climate Change is Most Important Issue Today," American Psychological Association, February 6, 2022, https://www.apa.org/news/press/releases/2020/02/climate-change.

5. Sarah E. Fredericks, *Environmental Guilt and Shame: Signals of Individual and Collective Responsibility and the Need for Ritual Responses* (New York: Oxford University Press, 2021), 5.

6. Randy Woodley, *Indigenous Theology and the Western Worldview: A Decolonized Approach to Christian Doctrine* (Grand Rapids, MI: Baker Academic, 2022), 41.

7. Andreas Weber, *Matter and Desire: An Erotic Ecology* (White River Junction, VT: Chelsea Green Publishing, 2014), 170.

8. Weber, 174.

9. Catherine Keller, *The Face of the Deep: A Theology of Becoming* (New York: Routledge, 2003).

10. Keller, xvi.
11. Keller, xvii.
12. S. Lily Mendoza and George Zachariah, eds., "Introduction," in *Decolonizing Ecotheology: Indigenous and Subaltern Challenges* (Eugene, OR: Pickwick, 2022), 3.
13. Mendoza and Zachariah, 4.
14. Keller, *Face of the Deep*, 238.
15. Bill T. Arnold and Bryan E. Byer, eds., "Enuma Elish," in *Readings from the Ancient Near East* (Grand Rapids, MI: Baker Academic, 2006), 31–50.
16. Michael Northcott, *The Environment and Christian Ethics* (New York: Cambridge University Press, 1996), 164.
17. Ellen F. Davis, *Scripture, Culture, Agriculture: An Agrarian Reading of the Bible* (New York: Cambridge University Press, 2009), 277.
18. There have been several incidents when ponds containing heavy metals have overflowed, covering farms, including a spill in Martin County, KY, in 2008 and a spill into the Dan River in North Carolina in 2014.
19. Tamara Shantz, "Not Your Promised Land," in *Unsettling the Word: Biblical Experiments in Decolonization,* ed. Steve Heinrichs and Jonathan Dyck (Maryknoll, NY: Orbis Books, 2019), 34.
20. Shantz, 35.
21. Vicky S. Balabanski, "Pauline Epistles: Paul's Vision of Cosmic Liberation and Renewal," in *The Oxford Handbook of the Bible and Ecology*, ed. Hilary Marlow and Mark Harris (New York: Oxford University Press, 2022), 241.
22. Balabanski, 245.
23. Balabanski, 245.
24. Balabanski, 247.
25. Woodley, *Indigenous Theology*, 41–42.

CHAPTER 5

1. L. Callid Keefe-Perry, *Way to Water: A Theopoetics Primer* (Eugene, OR: Cascade Books, 2014), 131.
2. Alves, Rubem, "Theopoetics: Longing and Liberation," *Struggles for Solidarity: Liberation Theologies in Tension,* ed. L. M. Getz and R. O. Costa (Minneapolis, MN: Fortress Press, 1992), 161.
3. Keefe-Perry, *Way to Water*, 62.
4. John J. Collins, *Introduction to the Hebrew Bible* (Minneapolis, MN: Fortress Press, 2004), 463.
5. David Abram, *Becoming Animal: An Earthly Cosmology* (New York: Vintage Books, 2010), 104.

CHAPTER 6

1. Abraham Joshua Heschel, *The Sabbath* (New York: Farrar, Straus and Giroux, 2005). First published 1951.
2. Norman Wirzba, *This Sacred Life: Humanity's Place in a Wounded World* (New York: Cambridge University Press, 2021), 144.
3. Wirzba, 146.
4. Whitney A. Bauman and Kevin J. O'Brien, *Environmental Ethics and Uncertainty: Wrestling with Wicked Problems* (London: Routledge, 2020), 112.

5. Henry George Liddell and Robert Scott, *An Intermediate Greek-English Lexicon, Seventh Edition* (Oxford: Oxford University Press, 1995), 392.

6. Liddell and Scott, 896.

7. Susannah Heschel, introduction to *The Sabbath*, by Abraham Joshua Heschel, xiv.

8. Wirzba, *This Sacred Life*, 145.

9. Susannah Heschel, introduction to *The Sabbath*, xv.

10. Abraham Joshua Heschel, *Sabbath*, 3.

11. Heschel, 3.

12. Heschel, 9.

13. Heschel, 14–15.

14. Heschel, 18.

15. Yoshifumi Miyazaki, *Shinrin Yoku: The Japanese Art of Forest Bathing* (Portland, OR: Timber Press, 2018), 10.

16. Miyazaki, 78.

17. This concept was first introduced to me by Janeen Bertsche Johnson, who uses this practice in her forest retreats. She first learned of the idea of beholding from Dan Schrock, spiritual director in Goshen, Indiana.

18. Abraham Joshua Heschel, *Sabbath*, 29.

19. "Forest Church," Communities of the Mystic Christ, accessed October 8, 2022, http://www.mysticchrist.co.uk/forest_church; Wendy Janzen, personal interview, October 3, 2022.

20. Janzen, personal interview, October 3, 2022.

21. Wendy Janzen, personal correspondence, October 10, 2022.

22. Janzen, personal interview, October 3, 2022.

23. Janzen, personal interview, October 3, 2022.

24. Janzen, personal interview, October 3, 2022.

25. Janzen, personal interview, October 3, 2022.

26. Bauman and O'Brien, *Environmental Ethics*, 119.

CHAPTER 7

1. "Renewable Energy," Center for Climate and Energy Solutions, data from 2010 to 2020, accessed October 23, 2022, https://www.c2es.org/content/renewable-energy/.

2. "Global EV Outlook 2022," International Energy Agency, May 2022, https://origin.iea.org/reports/global-ev-outlook-2022.

3. Barbara Rossing, "Waters Cry Out," in *Decolonizing Ecotheology: Indigenous and Subaltern Challenges*, ed. S. Lily Mendoza and George Zachariah (Eugene, OR: Pickwick, 2022), 44.

4. Rossing, 49.

5. "Groups and Projects," Transition Town Totnes, accessed March 25, 2023, https://www.transitiontowntotnes.org/groups-and-projects.

6. Michael S. Northcott, *Place, Ecology and the Sacred: The Moral Geography of Sustainable Communities* (London: Bloomsbury, 2015), 151.

7. Northcott, 152.

8. Transition Network, http://transitionnetwork.org.

9. "Our Story," Just Transition Northwest Indiana, accessed April 19, 2023, https://www.jtnwi.org/about-jtnwi.

10. Northcott, *Place*, 43.

11. Northcott, 45.

12. Northcott, 156.

13. Northcott, 109.

14. Northcott, 113.

15. Northcott, 121.

16. "Food Security in the U.S.," U.S. Department of Agriculture Economic Research Service, October 17, 2022, https://www.ers.usda.gov/topics/food-nutrition-assistance/food-security-in-the-u-s/key-statistics-graphics/.

17. "How Many Canadians Are Affected by Household Food Insecurity?" Proof Research Programme, University of Toronto, accessed April 19, 2023, https://proof.utoronto.ca/food-insecurity/how-many-canadians-are-affected-by-household-food-insecurity/.

18. "Heat Island Effect," United States Environmental Protection Agency, January 13, 2023, https://www.epa.gov/heatislands.

19. Martha Bebinger, "In Chelsea, Cooling an Urban Heat Island One Block at a Time," WBUR, May 12, 2022, https://www.wbur.org/news/2022/05/12/chelsea-massachusetts-heat-island-cooling.

20. Ched Myers, personal correspondence, 2014.

21. "Environmental & Climate Justice," NAACP, accessed May 26, 2023, https://naacp.org/know-issues/environmental-climate-justice.

22. "Carbon Footprint Calculator," United States Environmental Protection Agency, July 14, 2016, https://www3.epa.gov/carbon-footprint-calculator/.

CONCLUSION

1. Talitha Amadea Aho, *In Deep Waters: Spiritual Care for Young People in a Climate Crisis* (Minneapolis, MN: Fortress Press, 2022), 142.

2. Aho, 2.

3. Aho, 4.

THE AUTHOR

Sarah Renee Werner is communications coordinator for Central District Conference of Mennonite Church USA and pastor of Olentangy Wild Church. She is also a professor of ecotheology with PATHWAYS, an online theological education program affiliated with the United Church of Christ, and lead course reviewer for the Environmental Justice Certificate Program, helping to develop a series of courses to help pastors, laypeople, and theology students confront environmental injustice in their local communities. She has a PhD in religion from the University of Florida. She has served as guest editor for an environment-themed issue of *Anabaptist Witness* and has written several articles for the journal, a publication of Anabaptist Mennonite Biblical Seminary, Mennonite Central Committee (US and Canada), Mennonite Church Canada, and Mennonite Mission Network. She has also written for the *Journal for the Study of Religion, Nature and Culture*, the *Journal of Agricultural and Environmental Ethics*, and others.